Leaving Your Religion

A Practical Guide to Becoming Non-Religious

James Mulholland

To Jennifer,
my first reader
and the love of my life.

With many thanks to those who
read, edited and encouraged:

Rich and Barb McDaniel
Rob Smith and Jan Lesniak
Kevin Rose
Phil Gulley

Contents

This book is about happiness.

It is not about the momentary happiness that
ebbs and flows from day to day.

This book is about the deep satisfaction you experience
when your head, your heart and your actions
are in harmony.

If you are thoroughly satisfied with your life,
be it religious or non-religious,
this book is not for you.

Indeed, reading this book could make you unhappy.
Unless you feel some inner compulsion,
put this book down.

Of course,
since you read the title of this book,
opened it and are reading these words,
you may not be completely satisfied.

If so, read on.

"They must often change,
who would be constant in happiness or wisdom."

-Confucius

This book is for those
struggling with the decision
to leave their religion
and become non-religious.

When you think about your religious life
or your understanding of God,
if you wrestle with persistent doubts,
growing discomfort,
and feelings of sadness or anger,
this book may be for you.

If this has been your struggle,
what you think and feel
may no longer match your religion's beliefs.

While you can deny or ignore this disconnect,
eventually it will make you unhappy.

*When it comes to your happiness,
what you believe is not nearly as important
as your ability to live out those beliefs
with integrity and authenticity.*

If you are unhappy,
you may be ready to leave your religion.

"The only man I know who behaves sensibly is my tailor; he takes my measurements anew each time he sees me. The rest go on with their old measurements and expect me to fit them."

-George Bernard Shaw

Should You Leave Your Religion?

The following questionnaire will measure your happiness and satisfaction with your day to day religious life. It will determine whether you are experiencing a crisis of belief. It will help you decide whether you should leave your religion.

Please circle the number of each statement which best describes your **current** thoughts, feelings and/or behavior. Try not to respond with how you wish you thought, felt or behaved, or with what you are willing to publicly acknowledge.

1. I attend religious services...
    1. Every week with great satisfaction.
    2. Every week, but without much enthusiasm.
    3. Periodically when I feel guilty, depressed, lonely or otherwise compelled.
    4. Only on special occasions to support family or friends.
2. When I attend a religious service...
    1. I actively participate.
    2. I am bored or disinterested.
    3. I find myself irritated.
    4. I am surprised I once found it meaningful.
3. The rituals and ceremonies of my religious tradition are...
    1. Emotionally powerful and intellectually meaningful.
    2. Necessary acts of faithfulness, even when not personally meaningful.
    3. Meaningless though I sometimes participate out of nostalgia.
    4. Absurd and I no longer participate.
4. Most of the stories of my religious tradition are...
    1. Factual narratives with important lessons.
    2. Helpful metaphors about the values of life.
    3. Myths and fairy tales.
    4. Fabrications or exaggerations.

5. Many of the beliefs of my religious tradition are...
    1. Grounded in universal truth and divinely ordained.
    2. Helpful explanations of the world and how it works.
    3. Outdated and in need of change.
    4. Irrelevant.
6. I view the chief religious figure of my religious tradition as...
    1. Divine or divinely and uniquely inspired.
    2. The greatest human teacher.
    3. A good teacher who was wrong about some ideas.
    4. A humanly manufactured figurehead loosely connected to a historic individual.
7. Prayer is...
    1. An intimate communication between me and God.
    2. A sometimes comforting practice
    3. A time of quiet meditation.
    4. A pointless attempt to manipulate reality.
8. I would describe myself as...
    1. A passionate believer and follower of my religious tradition.
    2. A nominal member of my religious tradition, more by birth or upbringing than by intentional choice.
    3. A spiritual seeker.
    4. Non-religious.
9. God...
    1. Is the center of my life and the one I love and serve.
    2. Is deserving of respect and worship; powerful, but impersonal.
    3. Is a mystery I struggle to define.
    4. Is a human invention.

Please add up the numbers you circled.

Your score _____

_____

"The mind, once expanded to the dimensions of larger ideas, never returns to its original size."

-Oliver Wendell Holmes

What Does Your Score Suggest?

If you scored 9-14...

You don't need to read this book.

You are a deeply religious person and your faith is a source of great happiness and satisfaction. Your feelings and actions are generally consistent with your beliefs. You have a relationship with God which brings you comfort and guidance.

However, since you picked up this book and took this questionnaire, you are obviously a curious person. Be careful. Most religious traditions discourage curiosity. During the dark ages, Christianity actually argued curiosity was a sin. Unless you have more doubts than you're admitting, reading this book could make you unhappy or cause you trouble.

If you scored 15-18...

You may want to read this book.

You are in the beginning of a crisis of belief. You are finding the practices of your religious tradition less meaningful and having serious doubts about some of its central beliefs. Up until now, you may have assumed your unhappiness was your problem and not a legitimate difference with your religious tradition. You have probably made repeated attempts to regain your previous passion and faith with temporary success, but find yourself slipping back into doubts and questions.

Though you may still feel compelled to attend religious services, you find these services less fulfilling. You may have tried other religious communities looking for a better fit. A different community may have brought you happiness for a time, but you soon found your unease returning. When you have tried to share your discomfort with others in your religious community, you've been offered various solutions – pray harder, read more, question less - but none of these remedies have worked.

You may feel a little guilty about picking up this book and won't tell anyone you're reading it. If you continue to read, you may put this book down several times before finishing it.

Be gentle with yourself. This is hard work and you may not be ready for it. However, picking up this book suggests you're beginning to suspect the problem might not be you – that your religious tradition may no longer meet many of your needs or adequately address many of your questions.

This does not make you a bad person. You are simply being honest about your disbelief and discomfort. Remember, there is nothing admirable in pretending to believe what you don't. Of course admitting you're pretending isn't easy. Be patient. For many people, a crisis of belief can take several years to resolve. Hang in there, even when you put this book down. If your dissatisfaction continues, you will find the strength to return to it.

If you scored 19-36…

You should read this book.

You've been in a crisis of belief for some time now – the higher your score, the greater the length and strength of your crisis. You are probably not attending religious services often, or you are participating in the most progressive element of your religious tradition. Yet neither of these choices has made you completely happy.

You no longer believe many of the key doctrines of your religious tradition. You are increasingly uncomfortable with many of its rituals and practices. You have tried to hold on to a core, but that core gets smaller and smaller. Reading your tradition's holy writings no longer helps since you have serious doubts about the reliability of those writings. When you pray, you often wonder if anyone is listening.

You struggle with how to identify yourself. You make a distinction between religion and spirituality and may call yourself a mystic or a spiritual seeker. You may have read about or dipped your toes into other religious traditions. You may still believe in God, but your

6

definition of God is quite different than that of your religious tradition and difficult to explain. If truth be told, making sense of religion has become exhausting.

If your score is in the twenties, you have mixed feelings about your religious tradition. It has been a powerful force in the past. It is part of who you are. But it isn't working for you any longer and you can't pretend any more. You may feel sad and depressed about this crisis. You probably feel a void and real loss. You may even be hostile toward your religious tradition. You may feel you were duped. Sadness and anger are normal responses. This book will help you sort through those feelings.

If your score is in the thirties, your crisis of belief is nearly over. You've left your religion. You're feeling more at ease with your disbelief. You have accepted you cannot revive the passion and certainty your religious tradition once brought you. You may not have decided how you understand the universe and your place in it, but you no longer expect religion to provide the answers. While you may have few regrets about leaving, you still struggle with what's next. Where do go from here? How do you order your life? What do you need to explore? This book is designed to address those questions.

Regardless of Your Score...

You may have thought your struggle was unique, that you were the only person struggling with your beliefs. You are not. You may have assumed everyone else in your religious tradition was happy and content. They are not. Millions of people, both inside and outside of your religious tradition, are deciding religion no longer works for them.

"If you would be a real seeker after truth, it is necessary that at least once in your life you doubt, as far as possible, all things."

-Rene Descartes

A crisis of belief can feel lonely,
like blazing a trail in a wilderness.

This is especially true
when you leave your religious tradition.

You are disconnecting
from a community that
loved, supported and protected you.

You have been surrounded by people
who have looked, believed and acted much like you.

It is natural to feel
like a fish out of water.

The good news is you are not the first
making this transition.

Millions have successfully trod this path.
Many others are still on it.

You are not alone.

"Many people need desperately to receive this message: 'I feel and think much as you do, care about many of the things you care about, although most people do not care about them. You are not alone."

-Kurt Vonnegut

You Are Not Alone

Each year, over two million adults in the United States decide to no longer identify themselves with a specific religion. In 2012, according to the annual Pew Forum American Religious Identity Survey, over 45 million (20%) of the adults in the United States no longer claimed a religious tradition. This group – often called the "Nones" because they identify themselves as "none of the above" – is growing at about 1% each year and is already larger than any religious group in the United States.

Of course, checking "none of the above" does not necessarily mean you've resolved all your issues with religion. When surveyed about their beliefs and practices, many of the responses of the Nones suggest some level of religious confusion.

- 68% still claim to believe in God, though only 30% are certain God exists.
- 50% occasionally attend religious services.
- 42% occasionally pray.
- 18%, while they claim no religious affiliation, still claim to be religious.
- 37% call themselves spiritual.
- 32% say they don't believe in God, but only about 2% identify themselves as atheist.

Uncertainty about beliefs, diminished religious activity and identity confusion are all signs of disconnection from religion.

Depending on the strength of your crisis of belief, you might not identify yourself as "none of the above" in a survey. If you're still attending religious services, you probably continue to identify yourself with your tradition. Even if you've left your tradition, you may be like the divorced woman who initially keeps her ex-husband's last name. It's just easier than explaining your changed status. This ambiguity suggests the "Nones" are not the only ones experiencing religious dissatisfaction.

The Faithful Aren't All Faithful

Even among those who identify with a religious tradition, there are many struggling to harmonize beliefs and actions.

- 54% admit to seldom attending religious services.
- 22% are uncertain if God exists.
- 15% don't consider themselves religious.

George Barna found, using eight criteria for identifying Christian evangelicals, that though 92% of Americans claimed a belief in God, only about 8% believed all of the most basic tenets of Christianity. These studies suggest, even among those who identify themselves with a religious tradition, many are experiencing some level of disbelief. While Christianity has received the most study, there is reason to suspect this same disconnect in other religions.

This doubt isn't limited to those attending religious services. Another Barna survey found 33% of all Christian clergy did not believe in the resurrection of Jesus. Since 80% of those identifying themselves as Christians believe in the resurrection, there appears to be more disbelief in Christian pulpits than in the pews. Unfortunately, for those whose livelihood depends upon giving credence to certain beliefs, admitting doubt or leaving a religious tradition is even more difficult.

Based on these surveys, you can assume if you are still attending religious services, at least 25% of your fellow attenders and some of your tradition's leaders are probably struggling with their faith as well. If you are in a crisis of belief, many people around you, though they seldom admit it, understand exactly what you are going through.

"Believe those who are seeking the truth. Doubt those who find it."

-Andre Gide

Why Few Admit Their Doubts

Unfortunately, while many may share your struggles, it isn't always easy to identify those in crisis. Every major crisis in life is intensely personal. Uncertainties in your life create feelings of insecurity, inadequacy and vulnerability. You don't wear those feelings on your sleeve. In the midst of any crisis, you put on a good face and give the impression that all is well. You only admit your doubts and fears to your closest friends.

A crisis of religious belief is even more complicated. Talking about a divorce is no longer scandalous or shameful. Those grieving a death can find support groups. But, if you are leaving a religious tradition or abandoning a belief in God, there is still considerable stigma. Telling others you are non-religious or an atheist is a little like the gay experience of "coming out of the closet." This is especially true if you live in a rural community. Many who identify themselves as non-religious on anonymous surveys are far less likely to publicly acknowledge it. A crisis of belief can feel very lonely.

Don't be discouraged. Finding those who share your struggle or your evolving opinions takes time. If you leave your religious community, you will eventually find or create new community. You will build friendships with like-minded persons. The path ahead – though it seems solitary – is a well-traveled one. Though some return to their religious tradition after exploring life without it, most do not. Most discover a different way of understanding themselves and relating to the world. While this is seldom quick or easy, it can be incredibly rewarding.

This book is designed to ease the transition.

"The individual has always had to struggle to keep from being overwhelmed by the tribe. If you try it, you will be lonely often, and sometimes frightened. But no price is too high to pay for the privilege of owning yourself.

-Friedrich Nietzsche

The Purpose of This Book

This book is not a memoir.

There are many fine memoirs written by men and women who have successfully left their religious traditions. You may have read some of them. They can be very helpful when you feel as if you are the only one who thinks or feels as you do. If you haven't read such a memoir, you might find them helpful, but this book is not a memoir.

This book is not about theology or religious history.

In the midst of a crisis of belief, many delve deeply into theology and religious history, trying to understand their doubts and redefine the core claims of their religious tradition. Toward the end of a crisis, many will read theological deconstructions or historical studies that confirm their suspicions. This can be a helpful process, especially when trying to explain your new thinking to friends and family, but this book is not a theological treatise or religious history.

This book is a travel guide.

When you're safe at home, it's nice to read a travelogue, detailing the experiences of a brave adventurer, or to read a geology or history book about some distant land. Unfortunately, when you're in the midst of a crisis of belief, you've already left the safety of home. You aren't reading about a mountain. You're trying to climb it.

When you're on such a journey, you need a compass, a list of what to pack and what to leave behind, advice for how to dress and what to carry, warnings of dead ends, detours and potential disasters, and direction on what to expect along the road. This is especially important when you're traveling into the unknown and unfamiliar with no expectation you shall return home again.

You also need to be reminded to enjoy the trip. Every journey has its challenges, but it also has its joys. There will be uphill climbs, but there will also be those moments when you crest a ridge to discover you can see for miles. There may be instances where you leave things along the road, but also opportunities to pick up new treasures. You will meet exciting people and go places you've never dreamed. A good travel guide makes certain you don't miss any points of interest or wonder.

This travel guide is broken into three parts:

- **Part One: Leaving Home**
  An acknowledgement of the fears and losses that come with any change, however necessary or unavoidable. What must you leave behind? What should you pack?

- **Part Two: Walking Away**
  An exploration of the serious challenges you face when you begin to think and act in new and different ways. How do you explain your changing worldview? How do you order this new life? How do you become non-religious?

- **Part Three: Moving Forward**
  A celebration of the opportunities and possibilities for those who order their world without reference to religion or even God. What are the rewards of this approach to life?

In each section, you will also find questionnaires, reflection questions, quotes and other paraphernalia for the journey. Use what is helpful and ignore what is not.

As with any travel guide, keep this book handy. One of your early losses may be the central religious book of your tradition. Having another book to refer to may be comforting, especially when you can't talk about this crisis with others. Expect to return to certain passages again and again during the journey, especially when you get discouraged, or exhausted.

"Not all those who wander are lost."

-J. R. R Tolkien

Enjoying the Hike

Thinking about life as a journey is often the first step in leaving a religious tradition. While religions use the imagery of journey, most religions emphasize a destination – be it salvation, or enlightenment, or heaven – and demand you do whatever necessary to confirm your reservation. Once you achieve a certain status, happiness and contentment are promised.

This book is grounded in a different set of assumptions and understanding them may make the difference in experiencing a crisis of belief as a stroll in the woods rather than a death march. While these assumptions are embedded in every page of this book, you should probably hear them stated clearly at least once.

Happiness and satisfaction are usually temporary, requiring continual adjustments of thought and behavior. If you've read this far, you probably have doubts about the promise of permanent happiness. You know the experiences of life can challenge your beliefs, cause you to reexamine your assumptions and prod you to seek more satisfying answers. What once made you happy no longer does. If you are early in your crisis of belief, you may hope this present crisis will be followed by a lifetime of contentment and stability. Be warned. This is seldom the case.

Understanding life as a journey means never arriving. Once you stray from the safety of your religious tradition, you can expect life to be a series of shifts in thought and opinion. Having left the comfortable confines of cathedral, synagogue, mosque or temple, you've been given a tent. You will find many beautiful spots to pitch that tent, places of momentary happiness and satisfaction. Enjoy those moments of authenticity and peace, but learn to expect your wanderlust to return.

There is no need to denigrate the place you've lived in order to justify moving to a new place. This is not a journey from worse to better; darkness to light; or ignorance to enlightenment. These are religious concepts built on the assumptions of human inadequacy and of righteousness as a destination. If you hold onto these assumptions, you are more likely to join another religious tradition or create your own. The need to be right will cause you to build a shrine where you should have left a cairn. With or without religion, the need for moral certitude can make you an ugly person.

The clearest sign of this tendency is the temptation to ridicule the beliefs you once held and the person you once were or to belittle those who continue to passionately hold your previous beliefs. Resist these temptations. Be warned. Self-hatred, arrogance and hostility will spoil the journey and diminish your hope of finding happiness.

The surest guarantee of your future happiness and satisfaction is your past ability to create such moments. If in the past you were living your life with authenticity and satisfaction, celebrate. What you seek now is exactly what you knew then. If you now recognize you spent periods of your life living an inauthentic and unsatisfying life, don't beat up on yourself or blame others. Learn from that mistake. If others are finding fulfillment in those beliefs – and are not forcing them on you – be happy for them. You have no right to expect them to follow your steps. The best journeys are those where you choose your own path, looking back with fondness and forward with expectation.

When it comes to your happiness, what you believe is not nearly as important as your ability to live out those beliefs with integrity and authenticity. This book does not end with a formula for your specific happiness and satisfaction. While the path out of religion is well traveled, it quickly splits into many forks. Where you explore depends on your personality, needs and interests. This book can help you avoid unnecessary mishaps and dead ends, but it will not tell you precisely where to go or what to explore.

The end of this book is merely another beginning.

"One's destination is never a place, but a new way of seeing things."

-Henry James

Part One

Leaving Home

Leaving your religious tradition,
at best,
is like leaving home.

At worst,
it can feel like a bitter divorce.

Abandoning a belief in God
can feel like the death of a parent
or a close friend.

Religious beliefs, practices and relationships
have power, even after you find them inadequate.

They once inspired and thrilled you.
They gave meaning to life.
They ordered your world.

Losing them,
especially when there is nothing
to initially replace them,
is a real loss.

Acknowledging those losses is important.

"Leaving home in a sense involves a kind of second birth
in which we give birth to ourselves."

- Robert Bellah

The First Loss

Your first and greatest loss in leaving home is…home. Religions have thrived because they meet important human needs. They provide a community of care and support where you are surrounded by people who look, think and act like you.

This is comforting. You belong. You are loved. When you are in crisis – unless it is a crisis of belief – you are supported. If you were born into your religious tradition, you know nothing else. If you came to your religious tradition later in life, it was probably a powerful personal moment.

No one leaves home easily. When forced to leave, it can be gut wrenching. Even when you choose to leave, excited about a new adventure or place, packing your bags and saying good-bye is painful. You lose much that is familiar and comforting – the sounds, smells and sights of your religious life.

As uncomfortable as this can be, leaving a religious community is more than leaving a physical place. It often means losing the central construct for ordering your world, communicating ideas, setting priorities, making decisions, finding contentment and identifying yourself. You aren't simply moving down the block. You're moving to a foreign land with a different culture, customs and language.

Leaving your religious community is one of many losses. Depending on your personality and needs, some of these losses may be more painful than others. The following questionnaire may help you identify your deepest losses.

"All changes, even the most longed for, have their melancholy; for what we leave behind us is a part of ourselves; we must die to one life before we can enter another."

-Anatole France

Religious Loss Inventory

To identify the losses you are experiencing, please indicate which response – deep loss, some sadness, mild nostalgia, or little pain – best describes your **current** feelings about the loss (or potential loss) of each of the following beliefs, practices and/or relationships.

1. Your primary – and in some cases your only – community of care and support.

    Deep Loss   Some Sadness   Mild Nostalgia   Little Pain

2. Strong relationships with friends and family who continue to find your religious tradition and community satisfying.

    Deep Loss   Some Sadness   Mild Nostalgia   Little Pain

3. The weekly, monthly and yearly rhythm of life provided by your religious tradition.

    Deep Loss   Some Sadness   Mild Nostalgia   Little Pain

4. A clear set of rules and guidelines for ordering your life, setting your priorities and making tough decisions.

    Deep Loss   Some Sadness   Mild Nostalgia   Little Pain

5. The certainty that came with your religious tradition and its worldview.

    Deep Loss   Some Sadness   Mild Nostalgia   Little Pain

6. The shared story of origins, human history, divine intervention and corporate life supplied by your religious tradition.

Deep Loss   Some Sadness   Mild Nostalgia   Little Pain

7. The example of your religious tradition's founders and celebrated figures.

Deep Loss   Some Sadness   Mild Nostalgia   Little Pain

8. A deity to worship, connect with and thank.

Deep Loss   Some Sadness   Mild Nostalgia   Little Pain

9. An external authority to refer to when facing a difficult decision.

Deep Loss   Some Sadness   Mild Nostalgia   Little Pain

10. A setting for introspection and intellectual exploration.

Deep Loss   Some Sadness   Mild Nostalgia   Little Pain

11. A convenient vehicle for expressing generosity and offering service.

Deep Loss   Some Sadness   Mild Nostalgia   Little Pain

12. The assurance of eternal life for you and those you love.

Deep Loss   Some Sadness   Mild Nostalgia   Little Pain

13. A clear identity when describing yourself and explaining your beliefs to others.

Deep Loss   Some Sadness   Mild Nostalgia   Little Pain

14. An externally defined purpose for your life.

Deep Loss   Some Sadness   Mild Nostalgia   Little Pain

Please tally the number of responses in each category.

Deep Loss	**Some Sadness**	**Mild Nostalgia**	**Little Pain**
9	4	0	1

List your greatest losses in leaving your religion:

1.

2.

3.

4.

———————————————

"We must be willing to let go of the life we've planned,
so as to have the life that is waiting for us."

–Joseph Campbell

Counting the Cost

While you can never anticipate all the consequences of a major change in life, understanding what you've lost and how deeply you're feeling those losses is important. Leaving your religion is seldom quick or easy and pretending otherwise is ignoring a wound. The descriptions below will help you identify the seriousness of your present crisis of belief and offer some suggestions for using this book for healing, growth and reflection.

If most of your responses were of deep loss...

You are probably in the beginnings of your crisis of belief. You may still be attending religious services. You may not have shared your doubts and struggles with anyone. If you haven't left your religious tradition, reading through these potential losses was probably frightening. If you have already left, naming your losses may have been depressing.

This is normal. You may feel frightened. It takes courage to let go. You may be sad. You are leaving what has previously brought you happiness and satisfaction. Read the first section of this book slowly and carefully. You need to take time to mourn your losses and understand the legitimate needs those losses represent.

At the end of this section, you will be encouraged to return to this inventory and take it again. If there is no difference in your responses, you may want to read this section again, or put this book aside for a time.

You may even decide these losses are too severe, or you aren't ready to make a shift, or you can live with the religious dissatisfaction in your life. If so, live your present beliefs as authentically and graciously as you can. If or when that becomes unsustainable, you can always return to this book.

If most of your responses were of some sadness or mild nostalgia...

You have been in a crisis of belief for some time. You can probably remember feelings of deep loss, but that pain has diminished. You probably don't attend religious services any longer, but you haven't quite figured out what to do with yourself. You aren't frightened of life outside your religious tradition, but you have moments of sadness and nostalgia, especially around religious holidays.

You are beginning to accept your losses and explore new possibilities. Keep your most significant losses in mind as you read this section. These losses represent legitimate needs your religious tradition previously met. While your religious tradition can no longer meet your needs adequately, those needs remain losses until you find ways to address them.

For example, if you identified "a weekly, monthly, or yearly rhythm to life" as a significant loss, you may want to give special attention to the sections of this book that address the depth of that loss, the challenge of meeting this legitimate need for order and the possibilities for a new rhythm to life. Though you may not be experiencing pain presently, you may need to mourn and understand these past losses.

While you will probably find this section of the book more descriptive than prescriptive, you should probably not skip ahead. Unresolved grief can create obstacles to future growth and happiness.

If most of your responses were of little pain...

You are either near the end of your crisis of belief or have completed it. You have left your religious tradition and are experiencing happiness and satisfaction in being non-religious. You are probably reading this book for affirmation rather than guidance. You may be tempted to skip the first section of the book and move onto the sections on challenges and rewards. Resist this temptation.

In connecting with your losses and identifying the most significant ones, you may discover important clues to reordering and recreating your life. Ignoring legitimate needs because they were previously met through religion can mean living the rest of your life with unfulfilled desires.

Another common mistake is non-religious self-righteousness. When standing on the top of a ridge, it is easy to forget the difficulty of the ascent. Reading this section will remind you there are others still climbing. Recalling your struggle may keep you from becoming arrogant or obnoxious.

Regardless of your responses…

It is never good to leave home without saying good-bye. Since there is presently no formal way in our society for ending a relationship with a religious tradition, consider this section of the book an opportunity to pay your respects and honor what was once meaningful and valuable.

"Mostly it is loss which teaches us about the worth of things."

-Arthur Schopenhauer

The moment you identify
as the beginning of your crisis of belief
is seldom the beginning.

Long before you recognized your
growing religious dissatisfaction
and struggled with doubts and questions
you experienced loss.

The first ache came with the loss of
your passion and excitement for your religion
or for your relationship with God.

The pain intensified when
you couldn't restore your enthusiasm.

It became agony when you realized
the happiness you once experienced
might never come back.

The reason you didn't identify those early losses
as a crisis of belief was because
you were afraid.

When you are afraid,
you pretend there is no loss.

What You Fear

The first stage of grief is often denial. Faced with a deep loss, you pretend nothing is wrong. By ignoring the loss, you hope it will go away. Abrupt physical loss – the death of a loved one, a divorce, the loss of a job – is difficult to deny. A crisis of belief is usually more gradual and easier to discount – sometimes for years. You clutch desperately to beliefs and practices even though they've become hollow. While there are many factors in your resistance to change, the most powerful is unacknowledged fears.

This resistance is often driven by the fear of punishment. Most religions rely on a measure of fear to instill faithfulness. The first time you had doubts, you may have feared the wrath of God. You may still worry about eternal consequences. If you still believe in divine retribution, it is nearly impossible to abandon other religious beliefs. The stakes are too high. If you fear damnation, you should probably put this book down, repent and seek forgiveness.

Fortunately, a belief in divine retribution is usually one of the early causalities in a crisis of belief. You probably don't believe in the God of lightning bolts or in eternal punishment. Unfortunately, even after you overcome this primal fear, a crisis of belief creates other anxieties. These deeper fears are more difficult to soothe.

You may fear...

- Being rejected or ostracized by your religious community.
- Straining deep relationships with friends or family members.
- Living your life without the order your religion provided.
- Abandoning religious rules, commands and certainties without knowing what will replace them.
- Facing tragedy or death without the explanations and assurances of your religious tradition.
- Being identified by others as evil, immoral or selfish.
- Navigating life without reliance on a relationship with God.

These are reasonable fears. Leaving your religious tradition is not without consequence. People may reject and misjudge you. Life may initially seem chaotic and confusing. Take a moment and honestly admit your greatest fears in leaving your religious community or tradition. Write them down.

All change is frightening. The constraints of your religious belief, even though they chafed, limited your options and simplified your decisions. Your religion offered a single, open door. Leaving your religious tradition means closing that door and turning to face a thousand others – all unlocked yet unopened. This sudden freedom, though exhilarating, is still a leap into the unknown.

While this book can help you acknowledge your losses, anticipate your challenges and glimpse new possibilities, it does not eliminate the unknowns. It does not diminish the real pain, struggle and work involved in leaving your religious tradition. Every journey is different. For some, this transition will come more quickly or easily. For others, it may be more difficult. You cannot know for certain which it will be for you.

You must be brave, or at least patient. The ability and energy to face your fears is usually in direct proportion to your discomfort and unease with ignoring them. Though some people boldly confront their fears, courage is often the last resort of those who've tried everything else. Whether you are daring or timid, reading this book is a sign of your willingness to acknowledge what may be your deepest fear – religion isn't working for you any longer.

"Ultimately we know deeply that the other side of every fear is freedom."

-Mary Ferguson

Signs of Denial

Reading about fear does not forever resolve your anxieties. The journey away from religion begins with hesitation, many backward glances and occasional retreats. In response to your fears and anxieties, you may attempt to deny your beliefs are shifting.

You may be in denial if...

- You're making excuses for not attending religious services.
- When you do attend religious services, you spend most of your time daydreaming.
- You smile and nod in agreement when people make claims you no longer find credible.
- When you admit your doubts and questions, you preface them with "I probably think too much" or "I know I should have more faith."
- You feel like a hypocrite when you participate in your religion's rituals.
- When you talk about your religious tradition, you find yourself using the term "they" rather than "we."
- You hesitate to identify as a member of your religion.
- You confess to believing in God even though you've rejected nearly every common definition or description of God.

If you recognize your past or present behavior in these statements, don't be too hard on yourself. No one wants to admit what has been meaningful and helpful is no longer satisfying. When you flip on a light switch and the light doesn't come on, you flip it several more times to make sure the bulb is out.   A crisis of belief means admitting what once enlightened no longer does.

"When one door of happiness closes, another opens; but often we look so long at the closed door that we do not see the one which has been opened for us."

-Alexander Graham Bell

It is impossible
to resolve a crisis of belief
if you are unwilling to face your fears
and acknowledge what you will lose.

Try speaking these two sentences out loud.

**I no longer believe
many of the core beliefs
of my religious tradition.**

**I am not afraid of living
outside my religious community.**

If saying those words came easily
you have probably moved beyond fear and denial.

If it was difficult
or impossible to say them,
be patient.

You may be in the middle
of another stage of grief:

Negotiation.

"I believe that words are strong, that they can overwhelm what we
fear when fear seems more awful than life is good."

-Andrew Solomon

Your first response to a changing belief
is never acceptance.

While you may be unable to deny your doubts
you may still try to eliminate them.

You may try to believe harder,
hoping to restore the passion and certainty
your beliefs once brought you.

You may assume the problem is with you
and not with the beliefs of your religious tradition.

If making yourself believe again fails,
you may cope with, rather than resolve,
your religious dissatisfaction.

You may try to stay
within your religious community without
believing its central assertions or
practicing its key rituals.

For most of human history,
and in some parts of the world even today,
this negotiation has been the only option.

This is not true for you.

A Short History of Negotiation

You are not the first to deal with disbelief. After every proclamation of divinely revealed truth in human history, someone thought, "I doubt it." Unfortunately, since religion and political power have often walked hand in hand, voicing such doubts has been dangerous. It still is in nations where religious fundamentalism holds sway.

For most of human history, those experiencing a crisis of belief had only one choice. They kept their doubts to themselves. Doubters were allowed to remain in the community as long as they remained silent. No one was permitted to leave their religious tradition. You either belonged or you were expelled – sometimes violently. Books with titles like *Leaving Your Religion* were burned along with their authors. When one party holds all the power, negotiation isn't an option.

Today – in much of the world - this is no longer true. Leaving your religious tradition is a real and safe option. It is not, however, without consequences. Even in countries where there is a separation between religion and state, most cultures still reward religious affiliation. You can be elected to political office in the United States if you are gay, but probably not if you are openly atheist. This continued bias toward religious affiliation means you will probably negotiate with your religious tradition before you leave it.

A crisis of belief seldom results in an immediate abandonment of your religious tradition. You may attempt to revive your passion. You may seek to reform your tradition. Often you move from conservative to progressive religious communities as your beliefs shift. These are all attempts at resolving your religious dissatisfaction without leaving your religious tradition.

Sometimes this works. These negotiations allow you to remain within your religious community. They reduce your dissatisfaction to a tolerable level. Unfortunately, since you are reading this book, negotiation probably hasn't or won't work for you. Though futile, your attempts to negotiate are a sign of the real loss involved in leaving your religious tradition.

Signs of Negotiation

Negotiations are unspoken agreements or promises you make with yourself, or your religious community, or even with God in the hope of resolving or lessening your religious dissatisfaction. They are attempts to diminish the loss you are experiencing. You may be negotiating if...

- You attend religious services though you don't enjoy them.
- You repeatedly attend spiritual renewal events.
- You try one spiritual discipline after another.
- You've changed religious communities recently or repeatedly.

If these actions have renewed your satisfaction with your religious tradition, be happy. However, if these actions are driven by a crisis of belief, your relief from discomfort may be temporary. You are definitely negotiating if...

- You maintain your religious membership, but seldom participate.
- You've divided your religious tradition's beliefs into essential beliefs and optional beliefs and affirm fewer essential beliefs each year.
- You're more comfortable with the term "spiritual" than "religious."
- You've prayed, "God, if you exist, make it obvious."

If you find yourself in a constant cycle of doubt followed by renewal followed by doubt, you are probably psychologically stuck. This is not unlike the person who returns repeatedly to an unfaithful or abusive partner. Sometimes the familiar – even when unpleasant - seems preferable to the unknown. You may be staying in a dissatisfying religious community because you are too afraid to be alone or venture out. Unfortunately, this decision seldom brings happiness. Your religious activity grates and irritates rather than inspires and comforts.

As long as your religious tradition and community
offer something of value,
you will be tempted to negotiate.

By accepting the terms of this negotiation,
many can soothe or eliminate
their religious dissatisfaction
and find happiness.

Since you've read this far,
your negotiations with your religious tradition,
religious community, or with God
have probably failed.

You have accepted your religious
beliefs and practices aren't working any longer.
They are broken,
perhaps beyond repair.

This is a good reason to be sad.
Unfortunately, sadness is not usually
the first emotional response to deep loss.

It is anger.

"The truth will set you free, but first it will piss you off."

-Gloria Steinem

Two Kinds of Anger

In the midst of any significant change, there is often anger. Understanding the source or cause of this anger is vital if you hope to move forward. Take a moment and write down anything about your religious tradition or community that angers you. It may be beliefs, practices, people or past experiences.

There are two primary causes of anger in a crisis of belief. The first – anger that your world is changing – is normal and necessary. Even when you like the change, you may be angry you can't have the new without losing the old. Your negotiations have failed. Loss is unavoidable. Before you can accept this, you often need to rant and rave.

You may be experiencing this kind of anger if...

- After attending religious services, you find yourself dissecting and critiquing everything that irritated or bothered you.
- You are quick to point out the hypocrisies of others in your religious tradition.
- You publicly criticize your religious tradition, pointing out where it doesn't live up to its highest principles.
- When you pray, you spend lots of time yelling at God and demanding answers.
- You threaten to start your own religious community.

At the heart of this kind of anger is a wish that everyone in your religious tradition would shift their beliefs with you. If they would change with you, you wouldn't have to leave and there wouldn't be loss. Realizing you are no longer like them, you want them to become like you. Once you accept they are not to blame for your religious dissatisfaction – that you are the one who has changed – this anger will lose its energy. Your anger at them is an attempt to avoid your sadness at disconnecting from them. Review the instances of anger you listed, circle those caused by your sadness at losing what you've treasured.

The second kind of anger in a crisis of belief, though equally common, is more complicated and challenging. This anger comes from the recognition that the beliefs and practices of your religious tradition did damage to you or those you love. Your shifting beliefs have uncovered ugly scars or unhealed wounds inflicted by your religious community.

You may be experiencing this kind of anger if...

- You refuse to attend religious services under any circumstances.
- You leave the room when people speak about religion.
- You introduce yourself as an "ex" adherent of your tradition.
- You find yourself mocking the religious practices of others.
- You accuse religious leaders of intentionally duping you.
- You've become anti-religious rather than non-religious.

This kind of anger comes from injury rather than loss. Your crisis of belief may have exposed the negative approach of your religious tradition toward women, homosexuals, minorities, sexuality, science, or a host of other issues. You may be suddenly aware of how religion manipulated you with fear, shame and guilt or damaged your self-image. You may have been the victimized by a religious leader. If this is your experience, you are not evading the sadness of leaving home. You're fleeing from abuse. Review the instances of anger you listed, star those caused by past abuse.

If you have experienced abuse from your religious community, you've probably already found this book too gentle and gracious. It may have been difficult to name your losses or admit your religious tradition met any of your needs. While you are right to leave your religious community, you are dealing with a crisis of trust as well as a crisis of belief. You need time to separate the pain of injury from the pain of loss. You need to heal.

This book may not be helpful for you right now. Running away is not the same as leaving home. Until you deal honestly with the abuse you experienced, it will be difficult to identify your losses and legitimate needs. Like the spouse who leaves one abusive partner for another, if you don't find healing, you may even gravitate to another religious or quasi-religious community. This kind of anger can leave you bitter rather than happy and satisfied.

Sorting through the sources of your anger is important as you leave your religious tradition. Identifying personal loss allows you to grieve. Naming past abuse allows you to seek healing. Anger, at its best, should produce the energy necessary to change, accept your losses and resolve your religious dissatisfaction. It may be the tantrum right before you break into tears.

"Anybody can become angry — that is easy, but to be angry with the right person and to the right degree and at the right time and for the right purpose, and in the right way — that is not within everybody's power and is not easy."

-Aristotle

Anger is often a secondary emotion.

It is what you feel
when avoiding
a more primal emotion.

In a crisis of belief,
when your religious tradition
once brought you great happiness,
anger often masks sadness.

If your religious community loved and nurtured you,
if they cared for you in times of trouble,
leaving them is painful.

If they beg you not to leave,
it can be gut wrenching.

You're not really angry at them.
You're deeply sad.

The final stage of grief,
before you can move on,
is depression
and sadness.

"Those who do not weep, do not see."

-Victor Hugo

Sadness

A crisis of belief is not something you chose. It simply happened. You gained knowledge. You had mind expanding experiences. You met different people. You asked necessary questions. Your beliefs shifted. You did none of this with the intention of leaving your religious tradition or community. Once you realized the trajectory of your exploration, you probably tried to slow or stop the process.

However, when it comes to shifting beliefs, it is nearly impossible to believe what has become unbelievable. You cannot turn back even when faced with the uncertainty of what lies ahead. You will eventually find it difficult to understand how you once held certain beliefs so fervently, how they brought you comfort and satisfaction. Until then, both the memory of their power and the recognition of their inadequacy co-exist. There will be bittersweet moments.

You're experiencing one of these moments if…
- During a religious service, you realize you've become a critical observer rather than a happy participant.
- Someone joins your religious tradition and you envy their enthusiasm and certainty.
- You discover – without religion – there is little to talk about with some of your friends and family.
- You face a difficult decision and yearn for the days when "putting it in God's hands" was comforting.
- You can't quite discard your religious books or paraphernalia.
- You hear yourself singing the words of a song that – though no longer representative of your thinking – once moved you.
- You hear someone claim something ridiculous and realize you once made the same claim.
- You watch a sunset and wish there was someone to thank.

These are expressions of genuine sadness. Like leaving home, you recognize your need to move on, experience life in new ways and become a person independent from your religious tradition, but you're also aware of how your tradition formed and shaped you. There were – and are – many good aspects to what you experienced. Resist the temptation to denigrate all you experienced in the past in order to justify your new opinions. Though this may accelerate your departure from your religious community, it is neither fair to those you leave behind or to yourself. You wouldn't be sad if your religious tradition and community hadn't brought you happiness and satisfaction. You wouldn't be depressed if you didn't secretly worry you might not find such happiness and satisfaction again.

Remind yourself repeatedly that...

- You don't have to pretend this is easy or painless. Letting people know you are sad about leaving your religious tradition may ease the transition for you and them.
- The pain you are experiencing will lessen over time. However, you cannot speed its departure. If you are leaving a religious tradition after many years, you may experience an extended period of depression.
- Your sadness is evidence of your capacity for happiness. You will find this happiness again.
- You mourn the loss of what had value, but the valuable is not permanently lost. It is merely changing form or expression.
- Acknowledging sadness is a sign of mental health.

The sadness and depression you are experiencing is a normal and necessary step in moving forward. It is a dark interlude where the old no longer satisfies and the new has yet to appear. The appropriate action in such a moment is to pause – while waiting for the dawn – and mourn. If you move too quickly in the darkness, you risk stumbling in the wrong direction. Be patient. When the light appears, you will see the new path. Until then, embrace your sadness, shed a few tears and remember your religious tradition fondly.

"Don't cry because it's over, smile because it happened

-Dr. Suess

When you joined your religious tradition
friends and family gathered.
There was ritual, ceremony and celebration.

When you leave your religious community,
no one throws you a going away party.

There is no formal process
for leaving your religious community
It can be a lonely good-bye.

The following pages are designed to allow you to
mourn, celebrate and value
what your religious tradition provided.

Each section will highlight a specific loss,
acknowledge its significance,
identify the legitimate need it reveals
and suggest appropriate ways to cope with this loss.

The act of honestly acknowledging
and mourning the loss of your religious tradition
is the beginning of a happy non-religious life.

———————————

"Sadness is but a wall between two gardens."

-Khalil Gibran

Losing a Community of Belonging

While everyone experiences the pain of a crisis of belief differently, the most painful loss – ironically – is seldom a religious belief. Abandoning beliefs, once they are no longer believable or helpful, can be fairly painless. It is the loss of the community gathered around those beliefs that can be so devastating.

Your religious community has probably been your primary or - in some cases – your only community of care, support and guidance. You may have been born into your religious community. You have probably shared the keys moments of your life – rites of passage, marriages, deaths – with this community. Its meeting place has been a sanctuary in times of trouble. Some of its members have been role models or mentors. They have provided answers to many of the most pressing questions of life. In a sometimes lonely, hostile and confusing world, your religious community has been a good place to belong.

Belonging to any community has significant advantages. Communities are networks of shared resources and influence. There is safety and strength in numbers. Though communities have this pragmatic function, they are more than a business arrangement. Communities are also opportunities for love and intimacy. Your best friends are usually within a specific community. You often marry someone from your community.

Most importantly, communities form around shared beliefs. Faced with questions about human existence and meaning, communities offer you a set of answers about origins, ethics, purpose and destiny. Affirming and supporting this set of beliefs is the primary condition for belonging to a community. Communities help you organize your world.

Many religious communities offer all of these benefits with the additional claim of divine revelation, favor and protection. Your beliefs are stamped with God's seal of approval. You're taught God likes you and your community above all others. Not only can you depend on other humans to meet your needs, you can expect God to intervene on your behalf. You belong to the family of God. Those who belong to this family are promised its advantages in this life and the next.

Leaving any community can be painful. Without your community of belonging, the world can suddenly seem a lonely, dangerous place. You've jeopardized significant and real advantages. Who will celebrate your accomplishments and share your sorrows? Where do you go in times of trouble for resources and support? Who will provide guidance and counsel? To whom do you belong?

Leaving a religious community, with its claim of superiority and primacy over all other human communities, is especially difficult. If you were raised in a religious community, you may have been taught life outside that community was meaningless and unhappy. If you joined your religious community, you probably did so based on its promise of ultimate satisfaction. Leaving is nearly impossible if you still believe in the inferiority of all other human communities.

Beliefs in moral superiority or divine favor undergird many religious communities. Once you no longer share these beliefs or other core beliefs about origins, ethics, purpose and destiny, the glue connecting you to a religious community begins to dissolve. While this makes disconnecting easier, leaving any community is still cause for sadness. You are not simply abandoning certain beliefs. It feels like you are abandoning people you love and who have loved you.

For this reason, celebrating the advantages and relationships inherent to the community you are leaving is important. In so doing, you acknowledge the ways you benefitted and the real value of mutual concern, intimacy and shared beliefs. In most cases, you are not leaving because that religious community is evil, but because it is no longer the right fit for you.

Take a minute and write down five benefits and advantages you miss or would miss in leaving your religious community:

1.

2.

3.

4.

5.

These are not reasons to stay. They are losses to mourn as you seek places, people and practices that better fit your new way of thinking. You are not rejecting all the values of your religious community. Indeed, you are honoring one of the tenets of most religious traditions - belonging without believing is hypocrisy.

You are not leaving your religious community because it is easy, but because it is necessary. To borrow a truth from Christian scripture, "You cannot pour new wine in old wineskins." Your religious community may be able to expand to accommodate your changing beliefs for a time, but in many cases – especially when you no longer share their definition of God – your thoughts and ideas will eventually require a new wineskin. You will need to seek different communities of belonging. Until you find new places to connect, there is loss.

As you struggle with the loss or potential loss of your religious community, remember these important truths...

- Loneliness and guilt are insufficient reasons for remaining in any community.
- Religion has never had a monopoly on community.
- Millions of people have and are living satisfying lives without any religious community.

- If community is a deep loss for you, it is also a deep value. You will eventually find or create other communities of belonging.
- The best communities for you will be those that value a diversity of thought.

If you have not left your religious community yet, there are productive and unproductive ways of coping with your loss and handle the separation.

Unproductive responses include...

- Staying in your religious community and claiming to believe what you no longer believe.
- Remaining in your religious community, but making yourself and everyone around you uncomfortable.
- Leaving your religious community suddenly and cutting off all contact with anyone in that community. (This is healthy when a community is abusive.)
- Publicly belittling your former religious community and ridiculing its beliefs.
- Immediately seeking another community and claiming it is vastly superior to your previous religious community.
- Deciding you don't need community.
- Convincing yourself you will never experience community again.
- Returning to your religious community out of loneliness or guilt.

Productive responses include...

- Talking to the leaders of your religious community and explaining your thoughts and opinions.
- Writing notes of thanks to those who were most helpful to you in your religious community.
- Visiting your religious community periodically to reconnect with people you value.

- Acknowledging publicly the many positive ways your religious community influenced and impacted your life.
- Giving yourself time to mourn, center and reorient before seeking another significant community.
- Identifying the values – intimacy, mutuality, honesty, authenticity, integrity, compassion – you most appreciated in your religious community.
- Recognizing that abandoning religious beliefs does not require you to abandon life affirming values.
- Looking forward after each time you look back.

These responses enable you to treasure and sustain past relationships while also creating the space to freely explore new communities and friendships.

Though tricky, what you are attempting has been done by others. There are many fine memoirs describing the departure from a religious community. If the loss of community is especially painful for you, you may want to read one or more of these memoirs. Regardless of your religious tradition, rest assured that thousands of people have successfully left your religion, built a non-religious life and lived to tell about it.

"No man is an island, entire of itself.
Each is a piece of the continent, a part of the main."

-John Donne

Losing Significant Relationships

When you leave home, you leave people behind.

You may be leaving people with whom you've had long friendships. Some have been your teachers and mentors. Others have been your students and disciples. If you were born into your religious tradition, you are leaving people who have known and loved you since your birth. In many cases, all or most of your family is part of the religious tradition or community you are leaving. You may realize, as you consider leaving, that you have few friendships outside your religious community.

This is not unusual. Most people build their strongest relationships with people with whom they share certain beliefs. This is what draws people together. When your beliefs shift or you leave a religious community, you jeopardize these friendships. You sever one of the strongest cords binding you to these friends – your shared beliefs. While your family probably won't disown you, they may be very unhappy with you. Though some of your friendships may survive your transition out of your religious tradition, many will not.

Take a moment and list the relationships most likely to be negatively impacted by your decision to leave your religious tradition or community:

Don't be surprised if these people initially express disappointment, sadness or anger. They too are experiencing grief. They may…

- Dispute the legitimacy of your shifting beliefs, suggesting your doubts are unnecessary and any change temporary.
- Negotiate with you, tolerating some of your shifting beliefs if you'll maintain your identity with the tradition.

- Berate or scold you, insisting you repent and reaffirm your previous beliefs.
- Distance themselves, unaware of how painful it is for them to accept your new thoughts and identity.

This distancing – while it may be temporary – is often necessary as they adjust to an altered reality and a new kind of friendship. Remember, the person they knew no longer exists. Be patient. Don't expect them to immediately or easily accept your new identity or thinking. If this is or has been a long, difficult transition for you, don't expect it to be quick or easy for them.

It is easy to blame the loss of relationship on those within your religious community. You may be tempted to doubt the sincerity of their previous friendship. This is unfair. Remind yourself that your leaving has little to do with them and everything to do with you. The moment you thought differently than those within your religious community you began distancing yourself from them. You are the one whose beliefs changed. You are the one leaving. Being angry at them for not accepting or embracing your new way of thinking may actually be an unhealthy attempt at ignoring your sadness at losing their friendship.

You are choosing a path most of your friends and family have not chosen. It is important to understand why many will find it difficult or unnecessary to maintain a friendship with you. For many within your religious community, all you shared with them was a common belief system. For these people, your disbelief marks the end of relationship. There is nothing else connecting you to them. Their disconnection is practical rather than personal.

For others, your decision to think differently or leave the community can be unsettling. No community can survive for long if it keeps losing members. Your leaving is anxiety producing for those who remain. Some may interpret your decision as a rejection of them and be angry at you. In certain communities, those you leave behind will be encouraged to disconnect from you. One bad apple can spoil the whole bunch.

The separation from a religious community is complicated further by the need of those within that community to reclaim you. If you've left a religious community, you've probably been pleaded with, scolded, or even threatened. If you haven't left, you can expect these responses. If your religious tradition claimed superiority, they will find it scandalous that you plan to live your life outside the community. Many may be genuinely concerned about your well-being. To them, you have lost your way and risk eternal damnation.

Early in a crisis of belief, as you struggle, you may succumb to pressure from friends and family and renounce your changing beliefs. In so doing, you may even experience some initial exhilaration and renewed passion. The community may publicly celebrate your return. If this has been your history, it can be embarrassing when you discover your dissatisfaction returning. You may be tempted – for the sake of friends and family – to simply pretend all is well. Resist this temptation. Choosing the happiness of others over your own is seldom sustainable.

Friendships are worth maintaining, but pretending to believe what your friends believe is inauthentic. In being honest about your new way of thinking, you offer your friends the opportunity to relate to the real you. Some will respond. These are the friendships which have the best chance of surviving your transition. They may not choose the path you are choosing, but their greatest desire will be to see you happy, even if your happiness means loss for them. These relationships, while initially strained by your leaving, may eventually become even stronger.

"No person is your friend who demands your silence,
or denies your right to grow."

-Alice Walker

Losing Your Rhythm

There is comfort in the habits and routines of the religious life. Religious traditions are especially good at creating a daily, weekly, monthly and yearly rhythm to life. They provide order. You do certain acts at certain times on certain days. Milestones are celebrated. The seasons are given a narrative. When you are born into a religious tradition, this rhythm becomes ingrained.

While abandoning the deeply rooted habits and routines of your religious tradition may seem liberating, most people also find this freedom from the religious rhythm uncomfortable and disturbing. You may feel at loose ends, uncertain of what to do with yourself. You may feel guilty, as if you've neglected some responsibility. Regardless of your emotional response, it will feel odd, especially on the holy days of your religious tradition.

Some of this discomfort is nostalgia, but there is also real loss. Habits and routines have value. Most people do not do well with chaos. Religion offers culturally approved parameters for living. There are practices designed to focus, calm, inspire and comfort. There are rituals that accompany certain important moments. In a sometimes chaotic world, losing this structure can create a real void.

The habits and routines of life also give direction. As you navigate the joys and struggles of living, the religious routine sets milestones for measuring your progress. From baptisms to bar mitzvahs to ordination to pilgrimages, religion marks the key moments of life. A community affirms and supports you. Leaving your religious tradition means journeying without these convenient and comforting signs that you're on the "right" path.

A crisis of belief often involves the failure of this rhythm of life to work as it once did. The path no longer seems right. What once brought focus, inspiration and comfort produces discomfort, dissatisfaction and inner turmoil. Leaving isn't about living a life without order or direction, but about seeking order and direction in more authentic ways. This loss of rhythm, though necessary as you transition from one place in life to another, is temporary.

All of us have made such transitions before. When your education ended, you lost a rhythm that had ordered and directed your life for many years. No longer was life organized around semesters, classes, homework, tests, projects and grading periods. After your graduation – even though you celebrated this culmination – you probably also felt anxious and out of sorts. You probably missed the educational community, your teachers and fellow students and that rhythm of life. When September rolled around, it felt odd not to be back in school, uncomfortable until a new rhythm emerged.

Leaving your religious tradition is a graduation of sorts. You are leaving behind familiar habits and routines in order to begin a next adventure. For a time, religion provided the order and direction necessary for exploring your world. It identified the important questions and moments of life. It taught you the value of ordering your life in a way that exemplified your core beliefs. In leaving, you are continuing that quest.

Be patient. A new rhythm will develop. Give yourself time to catch your breath. You'll discover different ways to meet these needs. Some of this will happen naturally. Other habits, routines and moments may take some intentional work on your part. Until that new rhythm develops, you'll look back fondly on what was once meaningful. You should. Those habits, routines and moments helped create the person you've become – a person capable of different habits and routines, of giving the most important moments of life meaning and power.

"As long as habit and routine dictate the pattern of living, new dimensions of the soul will not emerge."
-Henry Van Dyke

Losing a Code of Conduct

One of the more common claims about the non-religious is that without religion and its dictates men and women quickly descend into moral depravity. While you may have once held this belief, you now know this is false. You are not leaving your religious tradition so you can be immoral. Indeed, your decision is probably driven by a deep commitment to honesty and authenticity. In leaving a religious tradition, you are merely ending a strict allegiance to a specific religious code of conduct.

This can still be difficult. A religious code of conduct is often deeply ingrained. It serves as a clear and concise set of rules and guidelines for ordering your life, setting your priorities and making tough decisions. It draws clear boundaries around acceptable behavior for the individual and the community. Indeed, the primary function of a religious code of conduct is defining who is in and who is out. Those who are in are faithful and good; those who are out are suspect.

Obedience, rather than moral reflection, is central to many religious codes of conduct. Those who obey the code please God and are rewarded. Those who violate the dictates of the code risk divine displeasure, community censure and possible damnation. Obeying the code of conduct is not primarily an act of moral responsibility, but of submission to God. In some religious traditions, the key question for the religious adherent is not whether a behavior is right or wrong, but whether an action adheres to the code.

Understanding this distinction is critical when leaving a strict religious tradition. Though you may have been taught otherwise, your religious code of conduct and morality are not the same. A religious code of conduct is merely one manifestation of a universal human need for fairness. Every community – religious or otherwise - offers such a code and those within these communities are taught these codes formally and informally from birth. All of these codes contain many universally applauded assertions. They also include stipulations which are not valued by those outside that specific community.

What you are losing in leaving a religious tradition is not your ability to discern and define what is right and wrong, but the corporate identification and approval that come with a specific religious code of conduct. Though your religious community – based on their religious code – may define your leaving as a wrong choice or even as evil, there is nothing immoral in leaving a community which no longer represents your worldview. Ironically, you will probably retain many of the most admirable dictates of your religious tradition. What you will abandon are those rules and stipulations that no longer make sense to you. You are asserting your moral independence and accepting your responsibility as a morally free agent

This new found independence may strain relationships with those in your tradition. You are defining yourself differently than your community. Even when you still abide by your tradition's code of conduct, it is an act of autonomy rather than of religious faithfulness or obedience. You decide what is right and wrong. In so doing, you will sometimes act in ways your religious tradition finds unacceptable. You will cease doing things they consider important or mandatory. Some may judge you deficient. However, you need not share their opinion nor harbor any guilt.

You are creating and claiming a personal code of conduct. The key question is no longer what your religious tradition teaches, what the holy books say, what God commands or what Jesus, Mohammed, or Buddha would do. WHAT WILL YOU DO OR SAY? You, rather than some eternal authority, are the final word. If claiming this independence is too frightening, you may not be ready to leave your religious community.

However, since you've read this far, you are probably ready and willing to take personal responsibility for your moral life. Here are some important cautions as you take this responsibility and develop a personal code of conduct:

- Rejecting your entire religious code of conduct is throwing out the baby with the bathwater. Sort through the rules and regulations of your religious tradition for what still resonates..

- Beware the temptation to systematically violate the prohibitions of your religious tradition. Moral independence means doing what you think right and not simply doing the opposite of what you were taught.

- Resist the urge to flaunt your new choices in front of friends and family who remain within your religious tradition. If kindness remains one of your values, respect the sensibilities of others. Do not belittle anyone for maintaining the code of conduct you once held.

- Inversely, do not allow others to shame or belittle you. Thank them for their concern, but stand your ground.

This confidence may come slowly. Religious codes of conduct are often followed by warnings of dire consequences for those who disobey. You may have moments of doubt, discomfort or even guilt. Listing the commands or admonitions of your religious tradition which retain the most value and meaning can be helpful. In keeping these commands, you respect many of the deepest principles of your religious upbringing while setting broad parameters for the way you wish to live from this day forward.

As with the previous transitions, be patient. Though you may miss the unambiguous clarity and communal approval of your religious tradition's code of conduct, being a free moral agent will eventually become a cause of joy for you. You are forever free to ignore that which makes no sense and empowered to act as your heart and mind dictate.

"I am free, no matter what rules surround me. If I find them tolerable, I tolerate them; if I find them too obnoxious, I break them. I am free because I know that I alone am morally responsible for everything I do."

-Robert Heinlein

Losing Certainty

Sigmund Freud argued religion was a human construct designed to calm the psychological neuroses and distress from living in a world fraught with random tragedies – natural disasters, the death of a child, sudden illness, etc. He suggested religion was a perfectly understandable response to the uncertainties of life and our own mortality, though a delusional and infantile one. When you are young and immature, when life is chaotic and difficult, or when your life experiences have been limited, the answers of religion often suffice. When you mature and your life experience broadens, many of the religious answers fail.

Whether you agree with Freud or not, his diagnosis was a back handed compliment to religion. Religion does give meaning to the meaningless and explanation to the unfathomable. It answers some of the toughest human questions – how did life begin, why do we exist, why is there evil, how shall we live and what happens after we die? – with confidence. Those raised in a religious tradition are taught these revelations about the unknowable and mysterious in story and song until they become accepted as fact.

For some, these answers serve and satisfy for a lifetime. For others – especially those who experience random tragedy – they can be a bitter pill to swallow. For those in a crisis of belief, these religious answers often become more troubling than comforting. A crisis of belief usually results in the permanent loss of certainty, even if you remain in your religious tradition or community.

This loss of certainty is one of the primary reasons many resist leaving a religious tradition. The human psyche is far more comfortable with order and certainty than chaos and ambiguity. Wrong answers are often preferable to no answers. Living your life without certainty can seem risky.

This desire for certainty is why many people explore other religious traditions before becoming non-religious. They hope to find better answers to the existential questions in another tradition. Others will be tempted to immediately move from a fervent faith to an ardent atheism, trading their certainty in God's presence for a certainty in God's absence. As long as you are replacing one set of absolutes with another, you are forever at risk of those answers proving unsatisfactory.

Looking back with longing on the simple religious certainties of the past is understandable, but their simplicity exposed their inadequacies. They often failed to account for the complexities of life, expanding human knowledge and even your own personal experience. A crisis of belief is about trading those certainties for ambiguity. Initially, this always seems a poor trade, but eventually you discover it takes far more energy to prop up inadequate beliefs than it does to simply admit you don't know.

Accepting some things are unknowable and many answers are speculative opinion is the beginning of wisdom. The more tenaciously you hold onto insufficient beliefs, the less freedom you have to appreciate the wonders of this complex and evolving world. This loss of certainty, while initially frightening or sad, becomes an invitation to explore.

You are not doomed to a life without meaning and purpose. You will always have strong opinions. The challenge will be holding them gently, aware they are tenuous and willing to lay them down if they prove inadequate. You can and should speculate about the deep questions of life - how did life begin, why do we exist, why is there evil, how shall we live and what happens after we die? – but you must do so with humility and curiosity. The goal is no longer certainty, but openness. The path ahead, though no longer straight, will never be boring.

"The whole problem with the world is that fools and fanatics are always so certain of themselves, but wiser men so full of doubts."

-Bertrand Russell

Losing a Shared Story

Religions, at their core, are epic tales. While they offer a list of rules and existential assertions, they package these codes and certainties in stories of ancient origins, divine interactions, human frailty and faithfulness and the past and future triumphs of the religious tradition. Taken together, these stories create a powerful narrative for those within the tradition. As a member, you are part of a company of saints who celebrate and reenact pivotal moments in the past. You are an actor in a cosmic drama, playing a role in bringing about some promised future. Weaved through the narrative is the assurance you belong and you are important.

This is a captivating message, especially if you were bottle fed on these stories. Your tradition's story shaped your personal story, forming and informing how you understood yourself and your place in the world. It often empowered, inspired and comforted you. Though – as your knowledge and experience grew - you probably doubted the accuracy of specific stories and details, you most likely clung to the broader themes of the narrative. Or, as some of your religion's themes became less compelling, you may have tried to redeem specific passages or accounts.

In a crisis of belief, one of the more complicated issues is relating to your religious tradition's narrative. There are several reasons for your attachment to a religious narrative:

- Stories are good. They offer easily remembered and understood lessons for living. Connecting to a shared story – be it familial, national, cultural or religious – helps you understand your place in the world. Those within a family, nation, culture or religion connect with, encourage, comfort and challenge one another in the telling and retelling of these shared stories.
- Everyone wants to belong and be important. Abandoning an entire religious narrative may seem like throwing your grandmother's Bible with its detailed, handwritten family tree into the trash. Living outside that narrative may feel like

becoming an insignificant cog in a vast, heartless machine. You risk losing more than a story. You jeopardize your sense of belonging and importance.

- Your religion's story is forever part of you. Once you have entwined your story within a religious narrative, you can never completely disconnect from those stories. You are a person formed and influenced by those stories, even if you now doubt or reject them.

- You were taught your religious narrative was "the story." All competing narratives were flawed and imperfect. Contradictory stories were labeled as evil. Disconnecting from your religious tradition involves accepting your religious tradition's narrative is also flawed and imperfect. It isn't the only legitimate story.

- The narrative includes you even after you leave. Most religious narratives include stories about what happens to those who stray from the prescribed path, vividly describing the dire consequences in this life and the next. In leaving, you play the role of heretic and apostate.

For these reasons, the sadness you experience in disconnecting from your religious tradition's story is complex. Though reading these stories as metaphor or myth can still be meaningful, there is real loss in accepting the world wasn't and isn't as your religious narrative suggests, that many of its stories didn't actually happen. If you are a romantic, letting go of the magical world can be especially difficult.

Sorting through the narrative, you find yourself facing many questions. What do you still believe historic? What, even if it didn't happen, still has meaning? What, if anything, can you still incorporate into your own story? How do you separate your personal story from the religious narrative? Even those who remain within their religious tradition often struggle with these questions. Those who interpret the narrative metaphorically are still a tolerated minority in most religions.

Though demythologizing your religious narrative can be painful, a deeper sadness comes in accepting you no longer share its story and themes with millions of people around the world and – more importantly – with many of your closest friends and family members. Since the story requires loyalty from its adherents, you have shifted from being a protagonist – one who believes and promotes most of the themes of the story – to being an antagonist – one who disbelieves and disputes many of the themes of the story. Your religious tradition's narrative is no longer the primary story forming and informing how you understand the world and your place in it. As you deal with this sadness, remember:

- You need not be embarrassed by your upbringing or participation in a religious tradition. Your history is a valuable part of your story and important as others try to understand you.
- There are many epic stories. At the very least, you belong to a family, a nation and the human race. You are important to each of those stories, as flawed and imperfect as those narratives may be.
- Your personal story has value outside the context of a religious narrative. You get to redefine yourself. While others may define you as heretic or atheist, as your story continues, you will discover identifiers that better describe your thoughts and journey.

Your story continues. It may not be shared with the same people, but it is still a shared story. Today, millions of men and women are making the same decisions you are making. While this emerging narrative is incomplete, it has all the marks of another epic tale.

"After nourishment, shelter and companionship, stories are the thing we need most in the world."

-Phillip Pullman

Losing Your Heroes

At the center of most religious narratives is a superhero. These figures are presented by the religion as unique and superior examples of appropriate human behavior, of stellar integrity and character, and of faithfulness to the principles and priorities of the religious tradition. Often they are bestowed with divine or near divine status as well as supernatural powers. Their words are understood as divinely inspired and universally authoritative.

Those within the religious tradition are taught to admire, emulate and even worship these superheroes. In most religions, the adherents identify themselves as followers of one of these heroes. While Moses, Buddha, Mohammed and Jesus are the more well known, even minor religious groups usually gather around some charismatic figure.

In a crisis of belief, your religious superheroes usually come crashing from their pedestals. You often conclude their divine status or supernatural powers are religious propaganda. You suspect they were not quite as perfect as you believed. You consider some of their words as culturally biased rather than universally applicable. You may still admire some of what they were reported to do and say, but you no longer consider them unique and superior to all others.

This demythologizing of your religious heroes can be distressing. Heroes play a valuable role. They help you set goals for living your life. They challenge mediocrity and inspire achievement. If you worshipped them, any diminishment of their status is distressing. It may feel like you've lost a friend and mentor. Mourning the loss of your heroes is normal and necessary.

For many, the most painful losses are not religious figureheads, but the religious men and women you encountered and admired in childhood or early adulthood. These people lived out their religious faith with authenticity, generosity and graciousness and made your religious tradition and its beliefs tangible and attractive. In becoming a person of religious faith, you probably modeled your behavior after them.

Once you leave your religious tradition, you will probably struggle with how to relate to these men and women. You may feel guilty for disappointing them. Or, you may resent the ways in which they indoctrinated you. Don't judge yourself by how well your beliefs match those of your heroes or judge your heroes because their beliefs haven't changed with yours.

Hopefully, what you most admired in both your religion's superheroes and your personal heroes was their authentically, how they graciously lived out their beliefs in the face of opposition and difficulties. Though your opinions now differ, you can still value this commitment. In a crisis of belief, you can follow their example even if you no longer share their conclusions.

Ironically, many of the heroes of your religious tradition faced censure, opposition, disdain and even persecution from the religious folk of their day. They often thought differently than the prevailing religious majority. They departed from the prescribed path. In many ways, they did exactly what you are doing. Be as courageous and steadfast as they were, but don't try to be them.

One of the negatives in having heroes is the temptation to mimic their lives rather than follow their example. Remember, you are a different person living in a different age under different life circumstances. You can never know exactly what they would have done if they were in your shoes. Becoming an imitation of them is an act of disrespect toward yourself.

Though the persons you admire often change as you age, most people will identify new examples of authentic and winsome living. So will you. These people will not be perfect or capable of superhuman feats, but they will demonstrate how wonderful and satisfying life can be, even without religious superheroes.

"If you meet the Buddha on the road, kill him."

-Lin Chi

Losing God

In a crisis of belief, your understanding of God nearly always changes. Though many of those who leave a religious tradition continue to believe in some greater power or personality, that understanding of God is often radically different than what they were first taught. For most, this transition takes place in three steps:

Step One: Refining Your Tradition's Definition of God
You begin thinking outside the tightly packaged concepts of God you were given by your religious tradition and question the assertions your tradition makes about God. You grow uncomfortable with frightening images of God and gravitate toward more gracious representations. You value and emphasize some of your tradition's narratives about God while ignoring or reinterpreting other stories.

Step Two: Expanding Your Definition of God
You start challenging ideas about God that don't match your experience or values. You reject the more dogmatic claims of your tradition about God. Though you are still most comfortable with your tradition's narrative about God, you suspect God speaks to all people and all religions reflect that conversation. You revise your own understanding and description of God, sometimes even borrowing ideas and thoughts from other religions.

Step Three: Redefining God
You shift from understanding God as a personality to that of a higher power or connecting force. You find yourself less willing to make definitive statements about the nature of God. God becomes less personal and more mysterious. While you still believe in God, your thoughts about God are so markedly different than those of your religious tradition you hesitate to answer when people ask if you believe in God.

Throughout these steps, you never really lose God. You simply abandon one understanding of God – which is no longer convincing – and replace it with another. In the process, you lose some emotional, psychological and social advantages, but you gain others. Indeed, in each of the these three steps, you may feel like your relationship or connection with God is strengthened.

For example, when you take the first step and refine your tradition's definition about God, you often lose an understanding of God which claims special protection, benefits and favor for you, your friends and family and your nation and divine displeasure toward your enemies. Though this shift can be unsettling, since you're gaining an understanding of God which is more compassionate, personal and inclusive, you seldom experience this transition as a loss. Your change of beliefs about God may feel more like a rebirth.

The greater challenge comes when you realize your journey may involve a fourth step, that your dissatisfaction may not be with a specific definition of God, but with the whole idea of God. Many never face this challenge. While it is unusual to reach Step Four without taking the first three steps, many find contentment – either temporarily or permanently – in these understandings of God. If you are satisfied with your understanding of God, skip the following paragraphs and move onto the next section. For you, leaving your religion does not necessitate the loss of God.

****

However, if you are more and more uncomfortable with using God language to describe your feelings of connectivity with others and the universe, or if you find the use of God language more confusing and problematic than helpful, you may consider a fourth step:

Step Four: Rejecting God

You realize the idea of God has become irrelevant to your daily existence. You no longer understand yourself in relationship with or connection to God. You suspect your past beliefs about God were mostly rooted in indoctrination, wishful thinking and societal pressure. Though you may still believe in some kind of connectivity, you no longer use God language to describe your thinking You either define yourself as agnostic or atheist.

For many, this loss of a belief in the existence of God feels like a funeral. Up until the moment you acknowledge your disbelief in the existence of God, you have lived your life as if God was ever present. God may have seemed as real as any other person. You probably spoke to God often and may have felt God spoke back. In times of crisis, your belief in God's presence was a comfort. In moments of great joy, it was God you thanked. There is often a feeling of emptiness when you first abandon a belief in God.

If you have made - or are seriously considering - this final step, remember these things:

- Give yourself time to mourn. Though you now consider God imaginary, this relationship was significant.
- There may be moments when you miss a belief in God and envy the continued faith of others.
- Be humble about your disbelief. Remember, a certainty about the absence of God can be as obnoxious as a certainty about the presence of God.
- If God was an emotional or psychological crutch, your responsibility is not to point this out to others, but to demonstrate your ability to walk on your own two feet.
- Continue to be open to the mysterious and wondrous. While you may not connect such moments to God or describe them in religious terms, they can still be transformative and mind expanding.

As with the first three steps, there are gains as well as losses in abandoning a belief in God. Eventually, you will experience the loss of God and God language as the opportunity to define life in new and exciting ways. Without a belief in God, you are free to explore and appreciate your own sufficiency, responsibility and capability to navigate life. God was a convenient placeholder until you took full responsibility for your place in the world.

"Question with boldness even the existence of God; because, if there be one, he must more approve of the homage of reason than that of blindfolded fear."

-Thomas Jefferson

65

Losing an External Source of Authority

Everyone begins life under the authority of parents, grandparents and other trusted adults. They teach, guide, warn and reward. They control, determine and command. They help you navigate a complicated world.

Early in life, religious leaders often join your caregivers as your most significant sources of authority. Credited with a special connection with God, you accept them as trustworthy authorities on the most important questions of life. Much of what you believe and do is based on what you've been told by your religious community and its leaders. Or at least it does until you have a crisis of belief.

One of the characteristics of a crisis of belief is the challenging of authority. You begin weighing your own experience against what you've been taught. You begin noticing inconsistencies and inadequacies. You're no longer satisfied with being told what to do. You want to know why you should do it. A crisis of belief can begin when someone – rather than taking your questions seriously - responds by demanding you submit to some external authority.

Being told you to believe "because God, or your religious hierarchy, or your religious writings say so" is never a satisfying answer. These religious platitudes probably weakened your confidence in the credibility and authority of your religious tradition rather than strengthened it. Your religious leaders, instead of offering explanations, may have demanded your submission to their authority. Do not submit. When any belief system, religious or otherwise, demands your unquestioned allegiance, be suspicious.

It is also normal to be sad. Your sadness comes in realizing the world is not as black and white as you once thought, that people you'd considered infallible were sometimes mistaken and that ideas you'd been taught were sometimes antiquated or wrong. This is a common realization. Everyone – unless they live a life of remarkable good fortune – faces some disenchantment.

Faced with the harsh realities of life, letting go of the ultimate trump card – divine power and authority – is never easy. The concept of a powerful deity who can intervene and alter the world is terribly attractive. Claiming God as your source of authority can be comforting and empowering. While you may bristle when someone demands your submission with the words, "God says so," you may also find yourself reassured by those words when facing a tough decision or emboldened by them when challenging the misbehavior of someone else. Even when you've seen the man behind the curtain, you may still want there to be a wizard.

This desire for some external source of authority often results in non-religious people replacing "God says so" with a different authoritative person, philosophy or worldview. Rather than accepting that all external authority is subject to error, some transfer their religious fervor to some new object of reliance and reverence The challenge, as you leave your religious tradition, is in trusting your own experiences, weighing the experiences of others and coming to your own conclusions. Can you resist the need for a trump card? Can you accept your personal responsibility and authority in this world?

This claim of personal authority may frighten you. There is an obvious advantage to relying on an external authority. In so doing, you escape the responsibility of both the success and failure of your beliefs and actions. In accepting your role as the final authority, you are the master of your fate. You, and you alone, determine your path. You, for better or worse, control your life. The issue is not what God says, but what you say and what you do.

"Anyone who conducts an argument by appealing to authority is not using his intelligence; he is just using his memory."

-Leonardo da Vinci

Losing a Place of Study and Service

Religions, when they are at their very best, value introspection and intellectual exploration and encourage service. Many of the greatest universities and hospitals in the world were founded by religious groups. Religions, with their focus on existential questions, invite their members to delve deeply into the mysteries of life. Most religions also incorporate some variation of the Golden Rule with its obligation to care for others.

Ironically, in a crisis of belief, while you may no longer find the answers of your religious tradition compelling, you may still appreciate its insistence that you address certain questions. Though you may not be motivated by the same sentiments, you may still share your religious tradition's emphasis on compassion. What you lose in leaving your religious community is not the ability to study or serve, but a convenient context for doing such things.

This can be a significant loss. You probably spent many hours studying the beliefs and writings of your religious tradition. You may have given up weeks, months or even years of your life to serve those within your religious community, or to reach out to those beyond your community. In a crisis of belief, you may wonder if that time was wasted, if the knowledge you gained was meaningless and the service you provided tainted.

This is not the case. Mastering any subject develops valuable and enduring skills. Caring for others changes both you and those you serve. Leaving your religious tradition is not an abandonment of study and service, but a decision to fulfill this commitment in a different manner.

Admittedly, the loss of your religious context for study and service can be quite bewildering. Where do you find others who are exploring answers to existential questions? What do you study? Who are your teachers? How do you continue to express your respect and care for others? What do you give time and money toward? As you struggle with your sadness at losing the comfortable patterns of the past and the void their absence creates, give yourself time and space to pause, reconsider and refocus.

If you choose, leaving your religious tradition can be like a summer vacation after a long, tough school year. Don't feel guilty for putting down your books and freeing up your schedule. Relax, reflect and play. Spend some time caring for yourself. Religion, with its emphasis on self-denial and self-sacrifice, can sometimes lead to self-disrespect. If you have been heavily involved in your religious community, this ability to balance the needs of others against your own legitimate needs may be your next important lesson.

Eventually, if you truly value intellectual exploration and service, you will once again find ways to explore and express these values. It will probably not happen through any one institution or context. You will probably become more creative and intentional. Your motivation will change. No longer will you study or serve in order to please God, or defend and expand your religious community, or assure your place in the afterlife. You will study and serve because that is who you are and learning and service make you happy.

As you discover these new patterns for study and service, be thankful for the ways in which your religious tradition nurtured your curiosity and compassion. While your religious tradition did not create this yearning in you, it did value and develop the necessary disciplines and strategies for fulfilling these desires. Unencumbered by the restraints and compulsions religion often attached to study and service, you are free to build upon all you've learned and experienced. Serve the world – not because your faith demands it – but in order to bring your deepest passions to the world's deepest needs. In so doing, you will "love your neighbor as you love yourself."

"Live as if you were to die tomorrow,
learn as if you were to live forever."

- Mahatma Gandhi

Losing the Afterlife

One of religion's great attractions is its promise that one day, after you die, you will be reunited with all those you've loved, that all wrongs will be made right, all pain ended and all questions answered. All religions, though the narratives differ widely, offer some hope of life after death. Indeed, most religions not only claim knowledge about the afterlife, they also guard the gates of paradise, defining who is fit to enter. The afterlife has both the possibility of reward and punishment, of heaven and hell.

Though the hope of life after death is nearly universal, explanations of heaven and hell often contribute to a crisis of belief. As you question the assertions of your religious tradition, you may ask the following kind of questions:

- If there is only one path to heaven, what are the odds I was born into the tradition that has it right?
- How can I justify the damnation of millions of people whose chief error was being born into the wrong religious tradition?
- Why couldn't there be a multitude of paths to heaven?
- Is the concept of heaven simply an attempt to soften the pain of death or rectify the injustices of life?
- Is the concept of hell a mechanism for religions to manipulate their adherents and threaten their opponents?

Often, in answering these questions, what you lose is your confidence in your religious tradition's neatly packaged explanation of what happens after you die. Ironically, in a crisis of belief, you may trade your certainty about the afterlife for a hope in one.

This is not an easy transaction. Many people, though they have long ago abandoned many of the beliefs of their religious tradition, are reluctant to let go of their tradition's claims about the afterlife. When facing death, you may find yourself returning to the narrative and language of your tradition. You may be reluctant to abandon an assurance about what happens after death. Unfortunately, the religious narratives around the afterlife may also create considerable

70

turmoil for you. Though the language and images may be comforting in their familiarity, the assertions may no longer be very convincing.

If this is the case for you, you may lose many of the clear words, unambiguous images and strong assurances you've found comforting when dealing with the death of a loved one. For many non-religious persons, when it comes to the afterlife, nothing is sure and certain. All that is left is hope.

This utter reliance on hope, though frightening and uncomfortable, can eventually bring you more peace than the religious formulas. It does not ask you to defend narratives that seem fanciful fairy tales, to determine who should be rewarded and who should be punished, or to require others to join your religion in order to secure their destiny. You can be hopeful while being intellectually honest and universally compassionate. When it comes to the afterlife, you can finally admit everything you think or say is either second-hand assertion or personal speculation. You hope, but you do not know.

This acknowledgement of your uncertainty about the afterlife also allows you to admit and confront the possibility there is no life after death, that perhaps this life is all you shall know. Considering this possibility is not the doorway to despair, but a leap into mystery. It is the difference between wishful thinking and genuine hope. If acknowledged, the prospect that death is the end can even elevate your awareness of the value and importance of this present life. If this life is the only one you have, it must be treasured, honored and fully explored. If not, what better way to prepare for the next life than by living this one passionately?

"Millions long for immortality who don't know what to do with themselves on a rainy Sunday afternoon."

-Susan Ertz

Losing a Religious Identity

Ironically, as important as a positive self-identity is to human happiness, many of the most significant ways you identify yourself were accidents of birth rather than a matter of intentional choice. You were born with a gender, a race, an ethnicity and a nationality. In most cases, you were also born into a religious identity.

Though some – as an adult – choose or alter their religious affiliation, the vast majority of the members of a religious community were born into it. Long before you were capable of choosing a religious identity, that choice was made for you. Your parents never questioned whether you should be what they were. They probably thought it their responsibility to raise you in their faith and guarantee your good standing with God. As a teenager, your religious tradition probably asked you to formally confirm and claim a religious tradition and – not surprisingly – you chose them.

Remember – in the midst of a crisis of belief – that your religious identity is largely the result of deliberate indoctrination. Nurtured within the safe confines and constrictions of this inherited religious tradition, its values, practices and beliefs eventually became as comfortable as an old pair of shoes, easy to walk in as you navigated the world. Your religious identity opened doors, allayed fears and created connections. When encountering strangers, it provided a clear way of identifying yourself and a quick means of identifying those who were like you. While it was not your only identity, you were probably taught to make it a primary one.

For these reasons, abandoning a religious identity can be even more difficult than leaving a religious community or tradition. Many, who have not set foot in their religion's places of worship in years, still identify themselves as adherents of their religion. For some, this may indicate some continued commitment to the tradition or its values. For most, it is often motivated by a deep discomfort with living without the only religious identifier they've ever known. A crisis of belief is usually the first time you've ever considered being other than what you've always been.

This reluctance to abandon your religious identity explains why so many who no longer participate in religious activities still claim a religious affiliation. In much of the world, a religious identity – if not a necessity – is at least highly advantageous. Losing that identity means losing those advantages and redefining yourself, risking possible stigma and even punishment. It is little wonder religious identity is often the last religious vestige.

However, as your beliefs and practices change, it will become easier to understand yourself differently. Eventually you will acknowledge your religious indoctrination – which will always be part of you – and redefine yourself. You will speak of being raised in the tradition without embarrassment or anger. You will experiment with different identities.

Redefining yourself takes time. You may try many identities – spiritual, agnostic, atheist, non-religious, humanist – before you find one that fits. Remember, as you struggle to redefine yourself, you are choosing – perhaps for the first time – to intentionally and freely identify yourself in relationship to the world. You are leaving your indoctrination behind. You are thinking outside the box, marching to a different drum and taking the path less traveled. When people ask who you are, you can describe yourself in all your unique complexity. In losing your religious identity, there is a void, but it is not an abyss. It is the necessary space for recreating yourself.

"Most people are other people. Their thoughts are someone else's opinions, their lives a mimicry, their passions a quotation."

-Oscar Wilde

Losing Your Religion

There are a multitude of purposes men and women claim as central in defining and ordering their lives. For some – religious as well as non-religious – the successful life is primarily measured in personal wealth, pleasure, notoriety, power or societal status. For those so motivated, religion is a means to an end. They give allegiance to whatever religious system best advances their agenda. They seldom experience religious dissatisfaction because they've never given more than lip service to the higher principles of their religious tradition.

You are not one of those people. You've always valued and sought a higher purpose for life. Indeed, one of your attractions to the religious life was probably its offer of a well-defined and principled approach. Your goal is not to die with the most toys.

In eastern religions – Hinduism, Buddhism and Taoism – purpose is often defined as self-actualization or awareness; becoming a mature human being. In western religions – Judaism, Christianity and Islam – the aim of life is often described as serving God; becoming a good and righteous person. In nearly every religious tradition, the intent of the religious life is to improve, transform and perfect the human condition. Religion assumes there is more to life than competitive self-promotion. Indeed, the problem with religion is not in its highest principles – which are broadly valued and applauded – but the tendency of every religious tradition to institutionalize these principles in such a way that they become a commodity to sell rather than wisdom to freely share.

Too often, though religion claims a noble purpose, in actual practice its prescriptions, expectations and commands suggest a less principled motivation. When you recall your religious activity, you may realize most of what you did served the purpose of perpetuating and sustaining the institutional needs of the religious tradition. While religions usually command their members to live moral lives, treat others compassionately and contribute to the world positively, they also expect their members to acknowledge, promote and defend their religious tradition and community as superior to all others.

This demand for brand loyalty is driven more by institutional necessity than malicious intent. You can probably remember a time when you found comfort and pride in your membership in the sole or superior path to true human fulfillment and divine approval. Excited by the power of owning and sharing a noble purpose with a larger community, you sought to convert or recruit others to your religious tradition out of genuine concern and enthusiasm. Naturally, when your experience was limited to one approach, you assumed what worked for you should work for everyone. Indeed, this assumption is what makes a crisis of belief so devastating. Suddenly, what you thought should work for everyone, no longer even works for you.

In that moment, you question the tight alignment between your desire for a principled life and the assertions and expectations of your religious hierarchy or system. You become aware of contradictions between how your religious tradition acts and some of the principles it extols. For example, though many religions stress the worth of all persons, most exclude some and diminish the status of others. You may realize some religious obligations seem more borne of ancient ritual and habit than of common sense or contemporary wisdom. How does shaving your head, cutting off the tip of a penis, immersing yourself in water, or circling a black rock really make you or the world a better place? Freed from an absolute allegiance to your religious tradition, you strip away the packaging from the core principles.

This process can be painful and frightening. You may not know anyone of high principles outside your present religious community. You may wonder if living a principled life is even possible outside your religious context, especially when those outside that context have been defined as lost or evil. You may feel guilty and selfish. As a person of high principles, you probably value loyalty and commitment. Isn't leaving a violation of these values? Coupled with your natural sadness at separating, it is nearly impossible to leave a religious tradition without some worry about losing your purpose for life.

Happily, what you lose in a crisis of belief is seldom your desire to live a life with purpose and high principles, but rather your confidence that you do this best within the confines and under the direction of your present religious community. For some, this realization leads to seeking another religious tradition or community that better enables you to fulfill your purpose. For others, this shift means living out your values in conversation with many religious traditions. For still others, you may simply abandon the religious context completely.

Regardless, leaving your religion doesn't necessitate a descent into hedonism and selfishness. Indeed, your purpose in life may remain remarkably unaltered by your departure from your religious tradition. You will probably retain most, if not all, of your core values. In leaving your religion, you're simply trading a map – with the path between cradle and grave drawn in indelible ink – for a compass. Your responsibility is no longer to stay on the straight and narrow, to follow lockstep in the footsteps of millions of others. You are free to explore this wonderful and complex world.

You've already begun that adventure. You've already strayed off the beaten path. You're probably referring to your religion's map less and less. Your path is no longer pre-determined, but don't worry. You will not wander aimlessly. You still have a purpose, an internal compass you're beginning to trust. Once you find your true north, where you go and what you explore is up to you.

"All institutions, every last single one of them, are evil; self-serving, self-preserving, self-loving; and very early in the life of any institution it will exist for its own self. So beware. True soul freedom can never be found in any institution. If they will pay you, let them. I did it too. But never trust them. Never bow the knee to them. They are all after your soul. Your ultimate, absolute, uncompromising allegiance. Your soul. ALL OF THEM."

-Will Campbell

Hopefully...

You better understand
why it is painful and difficult
to leave your religious tradition
or abandon a belief in God.

You've acknowledged, grieved and celebrated
what you've left behind.

You've thought about the stages of grief
and determined if and where you are emotionally stuck.

You have identified the legitimate needs
your religious tradition and community
previously met.

You have recognized gaps or voids
you need to fill as you journey forward.

If this is not true for you,
it may be helpful for you to return to page 21.
Take the Religious Loss Inventory again.
Check and see if your feelings have shifted.
Reread this section again.

Only when you're ready to leave home,
read on.

Packing for the Journey

The pioneers who settled the western United States often left home with Conestoga wagons piled high with every imaginable item they could bring from their homes in the east. Much of what they dragged west would prove worthless in their new surroundings. The Oregon Trail was littered with the debris these travelers abandoned along the way. A crisis of belief is no different. You'll pack more than you need.

Hopefully, the first section of this book – with its inventory of the losses – has allowed you to sort through your belongings and determine what you still must carry, what you can leave behind and what you must replace once you arrive in a new place. For each person, this process and its decisions will vary. Some may choose to travel light with only a few keepsakes on their back. Others may fill a wagon. Let no one tell you what to leave behind.

When it comes to your past beliefs and practices, carry whatever you need as long as you can. Whenever beliefs and practices become too heavy to carry, you can leave them along the road. If those beliefs and practices met important needs, you will eventually find different thoughts and practices to meet those needs. Don't allow the need to pack perfectly keep you from beginning the journey.

The following packing list may help you identify and make your choices. Mark what you can leave behind (LB), what you must carry (C) and what may need replacing along the way (R). In some circumstances, you may mark more than one box.

LB C   R   A community of belonging

LB C   R   Deep friendships

LB C   R   A daily, weekly, or monthly rhythm and routine

LB C   R   A clear sets of rules and guidelines for life

LB C   R   Certainty

LB C   R   A shared story

LB C   R   Heroes

LB C   R   A belief in God

LB C   R   An external authority

LB C   R   A place for introspection

LB C   R   A place for service

LB C   R   A belief in the afterlife

LB C   R   A clear identity

LB C   R   A noble purpose for life

Now that your bag – or wagon – is packed, your focus must shift. It is no longer on whether to leave, but on the challenges you'll face when you do. In the beginning, the path can be rough, full of twists and turns, steep inclines and multiple forks. The better you prepare, the less you're likely to turn back, tire or wander in circles. The next section of this book will guide you through your first steps. It's time to wave good-bye to your religion, grab your walking stick, pull out your compass and head cross country.

"The first step towards getting somewhere is to decide
that you are not going to stay where you are."

-Chauncey Depew

Part Two

Walking
Away

Leaving a religion is like
walking away from a mountain.

It takes a long time to escape its shadow.
It fills the sky behind you.
You're constantly aware of its presence.
You measure your progress against it.
You position yourself in relationship to it.
When life gets rough,
you may even turn back toward it.

But if you keep walking
the mountain gradually slips
lower on the horizon
until one day its highest peaks disappear
and you find yourself in unchartered territory,
with no choice but to explore
the lush and fertile world around you.

Once all the familiar landmarks are gone,
you may be relieved, afraid, excited and overwhelmed.
You may even feel lost.

Reflecting on what you're feeling
is vital before setting off in a new direction.

"Without reflection, we go blindly on our way, creating more
unintended consequences, and failing to achieve anything useful."

-Margaret Wheatley

Feeling Relieved

It is quite common to feel relieved when you first walk away from your religious tradition. You've finally left. You're no longer pretending to believe something you do not. Whether you announced your leaving publicly or slipped out the back door, you've quit participating in religious acts and practices that caused you distress or discomfort.

Take a moment and list four religious responsibilities or expectations you're relieved to be walking away from:

1.

2.

3.

4.

Resist any guilt you may feel in leaving these obligations behind. Your relief is confirmation these acts no longer met your core needs. If whatever you did was valuable to others, someone else will take your place. Though walking away from your religious tradition creates voids to fill, the list above is not of losses, but of the physical, mental and emotional space you've cleared for new experiences and opportunities.

Enjoy this relief for what it is – a temporary reprieve. Soon enough, you'll encounter new decisions, struggles and even pain. Becoming non-religious is not the end of responsibility, but the beginning of a new set of challenges.

"Relief is a great feeling. It's the emotional and physical reward we receive from our bodies upon alleviation of pain, pressure and struggle. A time to bask in the lack of the negative."

-Vera Nazarian

Feeling Afraid and Excited

Though relief is often your first emotion, walking away quickly evokes both excitement and fear. This fear is quite different than what you experienced when your religious tradition wasn't working for you. That was the fear of change and loss. The fear you experience when you walk away from your religious tradition is the fear of the unknown and unfamiliar.

Take a moment and list four unknowns about walking away from your religion that frighten or concern you:

1.

2.

3.

4.

These are probably legitimate fears. You don't know what to expect. You can't anticipate every challenge. A non-religious life will not be inherently easier or more comfortable than your previous religious life. Simply leaving your religion does not solve your personal issues. Indeed, walking away may have unintended consequences and create unexpected problems. Though carefully and intentionally navigating this new way of being can ultimately be rewarding, it is not a guarantee against future pain and struggle. All beginnings are hard.

Beginnings are also exciting. You can expect interesting encounters with interesting people as you discover interesting truths about yourself and the world. While there will be challenges and even occasional mishaps, there will also be moments when you experience life in ways impossible when you were tied tightly to a religious tradition or community. Though a mixture of fear and excitement is normal, dread is not. If you aren't a little excited about walking away from your religion, you probably shouldn't do so.

Take a moment and list four excitements you have about walking away from your religion and exploring a non-religious life:

1.

2.

3.

4.

Hopefully, you could list far more than four. If you struggled to name any excitements, you may not be ready to walk away. You may still be grieving. You may be leaving your religious tradition for the wrong reasons or at the wrong time.

Excitement is one of the best reasons to walk away. Those leaving a religious tradition often report being envious of the non-religious, intrigued by the prospect of living without a religious structure, curious about all they might be missing and secretly attracted to the thought of leaving. Though leaving your religious tradition usually happens when beliefs and practices no longer work, your departure should also be inspired by the possibility there are other thoughts and practices that might bring you deeper satisfaction.

Being simultaneously afraid and excited about the journey away from religion is normal. Remember, in the midst of that tension, some of your hopes and expectations will be naïve and most of your fears will prove unfounded. Don't allow those fears to cripple your ability to explore the uncharted territory before you. There are mysteries and wonders awaiting.

———————————

"To live in the world of creation—to get into it and stay in it—to frequent it and haunt it—to think intensely and fruitfully—to woo combinations and inspirations into being by a depth and continuity of attention and meditation—this is the only thing."

-Henry James

Feeling Unprepared and Ill Equipped

You begin this journey ill equipped and unprepared. You don't know where you're headed or what you'll encounter. You don't know what you'll need. While some of the skills you bring from your religious life may still be useful, many of the habits and practices of the religious life have little utility when you walk away.

These unhelpful abilities may include...
- Allowing others to determine your course of action.
- Adopting only beliefs validated by an approved institution.
- Memorizing a single story for understanding the world.
- Claiming as certain what is uncertain.
- Defending the superiority of your beliefs at all costs.
- Tenaciously believing ideas taught to you as a child.
- Taking opinions and ideas you've never experienced as fact.
- Waiting for others to meet your needs.
- Recruiting or evangelizing another person.
- Raising your children to believe exactly as you believe.

These are a few of the abilities that sustain religious institutions and are commonly taught to religious adherents. Though your specific religious community may not have valued all these skills, you probably still have some of these habits. Be aware that the skills you needed to thrive within a religious context are considerably different than those of a non-religious life.

This shouldn't be a surprise. You've probably spent much of your life being taught a set of skills specifically designed to shield and separate you from the non-religious world. You've been warned of the dangers of traveling or living outside your religious tradition. From the perspective of the religious, blazing your own trail can only end poorly. For the religious, someone else has already determined the best path. To wander from that path is to risk disaster.

There is risk in wandering. Some of those who depart from their religious tradition and community end up miserable. They make choices that bring them unhappiness and dissatisfaction. Some return repentant to their religion. Religions are quick to detail the travails of these prodigals. They are less honest about the many stories of those who – though ill equipped and unprepared – survive and thrive as non-religious people.

If you feel ill equipped and unprepared, don't be discouraged. You can learn new skills and adopt different ideas. Indeed, reading this book is the beginning of that transition. Don't be too hard on yourself. As you walk away from religion, you'll often fall back into the habits of the religious life. Fortunately, since those abilities aren't well suited for a non-religious life, you'll eventually discover physical, social, mental and emotional muscles you've never used. Though you can expect blisters and bruises, you will develop new skills and abilities. Don't be impatient. The best way to learn the skills necessary for walking away from religion is by walking away. In each encounter outside the religious realm there will be opportunities to learn a different approach to life.

These new abilities may include...
- Trusting your own intuition and inspiration.
- Testing ideas before adopting them.
- Holding in tension a variety of stories about the world.
- Living with ambiguity and mystery.
- Listening carefully to the opinions and experiences of others.
- Examining your unexamined assumptions and motivations.
- Being skeptical of what you've never experienced.
- Taking responsibility for meeting your own needs.
- Tolerating differences of opinion or belief.
- Allowing your children the freedom to think differently.

These are some of the skills and abilities you may find helpful for a non-religious life. Since every non-religious person determines their path, no single list can hope to anticipate all you may need. This is another reason you may feel unprepared and ill equipped. Unlike the religious life, there is no single direction, ordained approach or sanctioned path. You are free to go where you like. No one can equip or prepare you for exactly what lies ahead because no one else knows.

This is the adventure you are beginning. Your goal is not to quickly find a place where you feel comfortable, but to stretch your mind and heart. Remember these words from the introduction of this book.

"Once you stray from the safety of your religious tradition, you can expect life to be a series of shifts in thought and opinion. Having left the comfortable confines of cathedral, synagogue, mosque or temple, you've been given a tent. On this journey, you will find many beautiful spots to pitch that tent, places of momentary happiness and satisfaction. Enjoy those moments of authenticity and peace, but learn to expect your wanderlust to return.

What you need for this journey are the skills and abilities necessary to adapt and improvise, explore and examine, embrace and accept. There will be many moments on this journey when you will once again find yourself in unfamiliar territory, facing unexpected challenges and feeling ill equipped and unprepared. Initially, you may feel lost. You may hear the warnings of your religious tradition echoing in your head and worry that all their predictions of doom and damnation were true.

Such messaging, especially if you heard it for years, is difficult to ignore. Don't worry or panic. Don't freeze or flee. Look around you. Move forward one step at a time. Explore. In so doing, you will learn the subtle, but significant, difference between being lost and exploring.

"Do not follow where the path may lead.
Go instead where there is no path and leave a trail"

-Ralph Waldo Emerson

Feeling Lost

Most people do not intentionally leave their religious tradition and community. Many gradually drift away until they find themselves in unfamiliar territory. Some storm off in anger or pain. Others simply flee, stumbling from place to place, more driven by desperation than by decision, only stopping when they become exhausted. Regardless of how you left, there may come a time when you look around, wonder how you came to such a place and worry you're lost.

In one sense, you are lost. You are finally outside the safe and familiar confines of your religious tradition. You are far from the prescribed path you once faithfully followed. You are off the map your religious community provided. You are traveling where they warned you not to travel. You are also at the best starting point for a non-religious journey, for exploring a new land.

Though being lost and exploring may initially look and feel the same, there is a big difference. Explorers – in order to deserve the title - must go somewhere unexplored. The absence of the familiar and known – rather than being a cause for concern – is exactly what they seek. Indeed, until they reach such a place, they cannot begin exploring.

So it is with walking away from religion. What may look like being lost is exactly what you seek.. You are exploring life outside a religious context, seeking happiness and satisfaction in the unfamiliar and unknown, living out your understanding of yourself and the world with integrity and authenticity. Once you reframe your journey as exploration, you need not worry about being lost. Your comfort, security, peace and joy is no longer in a specific location, community or institution. Wherever you pitch your tent has the potential to be home.

This new identity as an explorer also allows you to redefine what you've been doing. You have not lost your faith. You simply have faith in different things, including in yourself. You have not lost your way. You have simply chosen a different way. You have not lost your appreciation of the mystical, magical and mysterious. You have simply surrendered the need to rigidly define, package and control such moments.

Ironically, if you recall how you felt when you were experiencing the most religious dissatisfaction, this was when you were truly lost. In the midst of your religious tradition and community, you had lost your passion, courage, integrity and self-esteem. Surrounded by the familiar, known and certain, you felt like a stranger and fraud. In reality, you did not lose yourself in leaving your religion. You found yourself.

It is when you find yourself in uncharted territory that you've truly walked away from the mountain. No more do you huddle just off the beaten path, watching others live the life you once lived. No more do you wander in circles, always arriving back where you began. No more do you hesitate and turn back when you hear the distant call of the faithful. You are finally lost – wonderfully lost – with no choice but to explore this new world.

If the thought of being wonderfully lost is incomprehensible, keep reading. If leaving your religion feels more like a necessity than a choice, be patient. It may take time for your fears to become thrills. Though the joy of exploring the unknown and unfamiliar comes naturally to some, it is an acquired taste for others. Take time to pause, examine your surroundings and get your bearings. From here on, no matter how you came to this non-religious journey, you have the option of carefully and intentionally moving forward. The following questionnaire will help you identify where you are and where you might be headed.

———————————————

"Not until we are lost do we begin to understand ourselves."

-Henry David Thoreau

91

Getting Your Bearings

The odds of reading this book at the precise moment when you're deciding to leave your religion are slim. It is much more likely you've left your religious tradition and community in the recent past and are presently struggling with finding new direction. To identify the challenges you face, please respond to the following statements with either "yes" or "no."

Yes No 1. I have told my closest friends and family I am no longer religious.

Yes No 2. I can explain why I've left my religious tradition.

Yes No 3. I no longer denigrate my religious tradition in order to justify my leaving.

Yes No 4. I no longer need others to understand my explanation or support my decision to leave.

Yes No 5. I am beginning to talk about my life without using religious language, images and stories.

Yes No 6. When talking about deep existential questions, I am comfortable admitting I don't know the answer.

Yes No 7. When asked my source of authority, I am comfortable relying on my own intuition or opinion.

Yes No 8. I am comfortable publicly identifying myself as a non-religious person.

Yes No 9. I have begun building friendships with those who are openly non-religious.

Yes No 10. I have eliminated most of the possessions and habits that might make someone think I am religious.

Yes No   11. I can meet my relational needs in a variety of places and from a variety of people.

Yes No   12. I have created new rituals and routines for celebrating key moments of life.

Yes No   13. I can articulate a personal code of conduct that does not rely on an external authority.

Yes No   14. I have found non-religious places to think critically and serve others.

Yes No   15. I have altered, diminished or eliminated the role of God in my life.

Yes No   16. I have adopted non-religious explanations for understanding the world.

Yes No   17. I accept my responsibility for defining my purpose and judging my success in life.

Please tally the number of "yes" responses in each grouping.

Statements 1-4: _____ of 4.

Statements 5-7: _____ of 3.

Statements 8-10: _____ of 3.

Statements 11-14: _____ of 4.

Statements 15-17: _____ of 3.

———————————

"Nothing is at last sacred but the integrity of your own mind."

-Ralph Waldo Emerson

Locating Yourself

If all your answers were "no"...
Make certain you've dealt with the issues highlighted in Part One of this book before proceeding. While this section of the book may still be helpful, some of the challenges covered here may not become relevant for months or even years.

If some of your answers were "yes"...
You have left your religious tradition and community. The more "yes" responses you made, the farther you've journeyed into a non-religious life. In general, the lower numbered statements represent early challenges in the journey and the higher numbered statements represent later challenges. Take a moment to review which sets of statements have the most and least "yes" responses. The descriptions below may help determine where you're comfortable and where you're stuck.

Statements 1-4: Separation
These statements demonstrate your ability to separate yourself from your religious tradition or community in a forthright, healthy and respectful manner. If you responded with "no" to some or all of these statements, you may be struggling with how communicate about your departure from religion. This is a common hurdle. You will want to read pages 96-115 carefully.

Statements 5-7: Language
These statements measure your comfort at abandoning religious images and assumptions. If you responded with "no" to some or all of these statements, you may be having difficulty learning and adopting a non-religious language and mindset. This can be confusing for you and for others. You will want to read pages 116-126 carefully.

Statements 8-10: Public Persona
These statements indicate your willingness to engage and identify as a non-religious person. If you responded with "no"

to some or all of these statements, you may still be uncomfortable publically identifying as a non-religious person in a religiously biased culture. While everyone is entitled to privacy, make certain you're not misrepresenting yourself. You will want to read pages 127-139 carefully.

Statements 11-14: Lifestyle

These statements test your success at creating a non-religious lifestyle. If you responded with "no" to some or all of these statements, you may be finding it difficult to meet some of your needs outside a religious context. This can be one of the more difficult challenges of becoming non-religious. You will want to read pages 140-163 carefully.

Statements 15-17: Personal Story

These statements celebrate your confidence as a non-religious person. If you responded with "no" to some or all of these statements, you're still struggling with how you understand yourself. Don't be overly concerned. Learning to be comfortable in your own skin can take years. You may want to read pages 164-176 carefully.

If all of your answers were "yes"...

You could probably write this book. Most of what you read here will simply affirm all the good work you've done.

Regardless of your responses...

Be careful how you read this part of the book. Though there is a loose sequence to the issues discussed here, resist the temptation to use this section of the book as a "to do" list. Remember, your unique journey may not include all these challenges or require every adjustment.

"Keep what is worth keeping
and with the breath of kindness blow the rest away."

-Dinah Maria Mulock Craik

You probably walked away
from your religious tradition and community
before you fully understood
your motives for leaving.

You probably walked away
before you could fully explain
your reasons for doing so.

You probably walked away
while dealing with grief, sadness or anger;
needing to justify your decision to leave
by blaming others.

As long as you're blaming others,
you are not taking full responsibility for
your decision to walk away.

One of the early challenges
in walking away from your religion
is in understanding and communicating,
to yourself and to others,
why you are walking away.

When you can finally
state your reasons for leaving
clearly, calmly and without rancor,
you will truly be free to explore
without looking back.

Deciding When and How To Tell Others
You Are No Longer Religious

When you leave your religious tradition and community, there are two early and corresponding challenges. The first is in understanding why you left. The second is in learning when and how and with whom to share this very personal self-awareness. While you began walking away long before you could fully communicate your reasons for leaving, those who can eventually understand and articulate their motivation usually find the leaving and walking away much easier

Understanding Why

The first explanations you give for why you're leaving your religious tradition or community – even when your leaving is thoughtfully considered - are usually incorrect or incomplete. This is probably unavoidable. There is seldom a single cause and usually a multitude of contributing factors. It takes time to sort through all the possible reasons and settle on what best explains your decision. In this process, how you understand and explain your departure may shift repeatedly.

Don't be embarrassed by this lack of clarity or consistency. The reasons people remain in a religious tradition or community are equally complicated and changing. Your first responsibility is not to provide answers that satisfy those you are leaving behind, but determining why walking away from your religious tradition feels so necessary and important to you. This is a key distinction. Your goal is not to justify your decision, but to understand it. Once you understand your reasoning – or your compulsion – you can better determine when and with whom and how you share this information.

Though there are a great number of legitimate reasons for leaving a religious tradition or community, some are more empowering than others. The following are common explanations for leaving with commentary on why they are inadequate as a primary rationale for becoming non-religious.

- "My religious community, religious leaders, or fellow followers were abusive to me.

  This is unfortunate and you were right to leave, but leaving a community because its leaders or members were ugly people is not the same as deciding to become non-religious.

- "The people in my religious tradition were all hypocrites."

  This is not only untrue, it is unfair. Some people live out the highest principles and values of their religious tradition beautifully. Expecting anyone to live out their beliefs perfectly is a standard you cannot meet.

- "My religion was teaching ideas I couldn't believe or accept."

  Though this may be true, it implies they changed rather than you. They are probably teaching the same ideas you once believed and accepted wholeheartedly. They are not the one who changed.

- "My religious community wouldn't tolerate my differing beliefs."

  And rightly so. If your opinions became radically different than their creeds and conventions, they were within their rights to discipline you or ask you to leave. Being kicked out is not the same as walking away.

Each of these statements – and others like them – share a common flaw. They place the responsibility for leaving on someone other than you. Though the statements above may have contributed to your decision, blaming your religious tradition or community isn't helpful. Blaming seeks a justification and you don't have to justify your decision to become non-religious.

Ideally, becoming non-religious should be an action and not a reaction. Whatever explanation you finally settle upon, it should begin with the pronoun "I" and continue with a positive and active verb. I changed. I discovered. I learned. I needed. I decided.

Take a moment and explain in one sentence – using an "I" statement – why you've left your religious tradition:

Don't be frustrated if you dislike this version. As stated above, it may take many attempts for you to finally articulate an explanation that deeply resonates and satisfies. Until you reach that point, you may preface any explanation with the disclaimer, "As I presently understand myself..." You may want to avoid giving any explanation at all. Ultimately, when and if you choose to explain yourself is completely up to you.

Choosing When

The best time to begin sharing your explanation for becoming non-religious is when you feel comfortable – comfortable with your understanding, comfortable with your conversation partner or questioner and comfortable with your ability to share your understanding gently and kindly. Unfortunately, you may feel compelled internally or by others to offer an explanation long before you're completely ready. Handling each of these situations can be challenging.

When faced with the inner compulsion to explain yourself, ask yourself these three simple questions:

1. Am I trying to blame or justify?
   -If so, try to resist.
   -If not, consider the next question.

2. Do I need this person or group's validation?
   -If so, try to resist.
   -If not, consider the next question.

3. Will my explanation ease pain or cause it?
   -Causing pain unnecessarily is never appropriate. If your explanation will cause pain, try to resist.
   -Easing pain is always kind. If your explanation will ease pain, try to explain yourself.

You may still feel compelled to explain or justify your decision to leave, but by asking such questions you will hopefully be more aware of what is going on inside of you. Sharing your personal journey indiscriminately can be a sign of your own insecurity. It can also be a symptom of the early enthusiasm you experience with any new passion.

Excited about your decision to leave, you may think everyone else should make it. Be careful. A non-religious zealot is as unpleasant as a religious one. Remember, most people don't care what you think. Others will only be irritated. The best moments for sharing your journey or explanation are when you are asked.

And you will be asked. Whether you leave in a rush or gradually disconnect, someone – a religious leader, a close friend, a family member – will eventually ask why you're no longer participating in your religious community. Initially, you may give excuses rather than an explanation. As it becomes more obvious you're walking away, sooner or later someone will corner you and inquire about your faith. Remember, they are usually legitimately concerned. In such moments, your challenge is deciding whether you are ready and able to share your journey with this person.

Choosing Who

Not everyone deserves an explanation. Religions are voluntary associations. You are not required to register or justify your departure. Indeed, many religious communities will continue to claim you as a member whether you participate or not. Though you may choose to notify your religious community of your departure, this is not necessary.

Eventually, you may receive some official inquiry from a religious leader. This inquiry is often routine and the questioner is fulfilling a task. Offering a detailed critique of the tradition or community is unnecessary. Don't bare your soul. It is perfectly acceptable to say, "I've decided to no longer attend or participate" and leave it at that.

The more difficult conversations involve friends and family, people whom you have interacted with through your religious tradition or community. They may be parents or grandparents. They may be respected friends. They may even be a spouse or one of your children. They may come to you out of genuine concern, deep angst, or confusion and disappointment.

The pain involved in such conversations is why some avoid acknowledging their leave-taking, even to themselves. Some give excuses – illness, work, transportation – for leaving their community, camouflaging the deeper reasons for their lack of participation. Others may blame some circumstance or person for their disconnect, thereby escaping personal reflection or responsibility and leaving friends and family with the hope of their return. Though such methods can lessen your religious dissatisfaction, they are ultimately dishonest.

While who you share with is your decision, completely avoiding conversations about why you left can be inhibiting. It limits where you can walk, what you can say, what you can do and who you can do it with. Being honest with others, even if it discomforts them, is a sign of respect and a necessity for integrity. It is also difficult. It isn't easy to walk away when significant people in your life come running after you, begging you to return and asking for some explanation.

When faced with the request to explain yourself, ask yourself the following questions:

1. Is this a person whose relationship I value and wish to sustain?
    -If not, it is entirely appropriate to decline their request. Tell them you have personal reasons for your decision and that you are not willing or interested in sharing those reasons with them.
    -If so, consider the next question.

2. Am I able to offer a coherent explanation?
   -If not, admit your lack of clarity and ask them to be patient. Promise to be as open and honest about your journey as you are able.
   -If so, consider the next question.

3. Will my explanation ease pain or cause it?
   -If your explanation will ease pain, offer it.
   -If your explanation will cause pain, offer it as gently and kindly as you can. Close friends and family deserve an explanation even if it will be difficult for them to accept.

No explanation will satisfy everyone. Be prepared to lose some friends and be estranged from some family. Other relationships may be diminished. Some may reject your explanation for leaving and substitute it with one they find more palatable. But – if you are patient, honest and kind – many relationships can emerge stronger and more authentic. Your non-religious life does not require disconnecting from your religious friends. It only requires you to be honest with them.

Flip back to page 48 and review the significant relationships you feared losing in leaving your religious tradition. These are probably people who deserve an explanation. On the following page, list both those to whom you wish to give an explanation and those to whom you do not.

Deserving   Undeserving

There is one additional situation you may face when you walk away from a religious community. You may have acquaintances – within your religious community or outside it – who express sudden interest in your lack of religious participation or your new thinking. When it is someone within your religious community, they may see your leaving as a challenge or a threat. Giving them an explanation often results in an attack or debate. If this occurs, disconnect quickly. You don't deserve to be ambushed, especially when you're still unsteady on your feet.

However, aggression is not always the motive when an acquaintance is inquisitive. Sometimes people - within or outside your religious community - are dealing with many of the same doubts and struggles you're facing. They ask in hope of finding someone who understands. The easiest way to separate the obnoxious from the legitimately curious is with a question of your own – "Why do you ask?" If the response is ill motivated, end the conversation. If genuine, you may have found a kindred spirit.

Explaining yourself, especially when you're still formulating an explanation, is always a challenge. Sometimes the first person you tell should be someone with whom you have no emotional attachment – a counselor, a casual acquaintance, or even a stranger. This gives you the opportunity to try out different words and approaches without the fear of damaging a deep relationship or getting something wrong. Using an anonymous internet forum can also be a good place to figure out how to explain yourself.

Choosing How

Once you sort out the why, when and who of explaining your decision to walk away, you are still left with the how. How do you explain a decision that may seem unnecessary to some, disastrous to others and incomprehensible to many? How do you guard your autonomy while respecting the autonomy of others? Though – as with most choices on this journey – there isn't one prescribed way, there are some techniques you should probably avoid.

Generally, it is not wise to...

- Announce your leaving in a religious service or on Facebook or Twitter. This modern equivalent of nailing your confessions to the door is a good way to burn bridges, but may make later conversations more difficult.

- Make any public declarations before you've shared your decision with significant others. Let them hear it from you personally when possible.

- Critique or ridicule your religious community, its adherents and its beliefs. Your opinions will probably seem ridiculous to them.

- Present your opinions as certainties. They are not.

- Suggest your thinking is more enlightened. Being authentic is more than adequate.

- Imply others should make the same choices you are making. If you are seeking validation, you are still not taking full responsibility for walking away.

It is far better to...

- Talk one on one with people you suspect may find your decision difficult.

- Highlight what you still value about your religious upbringing and experience, acknowledging it once satisfied.

- Admit your doubts and fears in walking away. Don't make your decision seem easy or simple.

- Confess your uncertainties about the path ahead and the questions you haven't answered.

- Reserve the right to change your explanation as you better understand your motives and needs.

- Encourage and celebrate personal authenticity – whether in a religious or non-religious context.

Your goal in communicating your decision to walk away from your religious tradition is to be clear and kind. Avoid the temptation to give more detail than necessary. Often, it is sufficient to say, "My religion wasn't working for me any longer." For many, this will be sufficient. For those who need more, let them ask their pressing questions. Answer what you can. Leave unanswered what is yet unclear to you.

In the end, how you present yourself may be as important as what you think. If you seem defensive, critical, arrogant, timid, or uncomfortable, this says far more about you than those with whom you're engaging. If you seem at peace with your decision, the anxiety of those around you will quickly diminish. This is, of course, much easier said than done. Be patient. Every time you explain your decision to someone it will become clearer and easier to express. Indeed, there may come a day when you'll wonder why you ever felt the need to explain it at all. You are who you are and that is enough.

"Integrity is telling myself the truth.
And honesty is telling the truth to other people."

-Spencer Johnson

As you move farther and farther
from your religious tradition,
there will be fewer demands for an explanation.

People will adjust to your
new thinking, lifestyle and identity
or they will write you off.
You have little control over either response.

This is good.
You need to focus your attention
more on walking and less on talking.
Those who talk and walk
often trip.

When you venture into uncharted territory,
the path isn't always clear or unobstructed.
There will be…
dead ends, time consuming detours
and occasional falls.

When you walk the well-worn path,
your steps are certain.

When you head cross country,
it's wise to navigate more carefully
and step more lightly.

Avoiding Early Pitfalls

Every journey has its hazards and the journey away from religion is no different. Even when you walk carefully, you'll take a tumble now and again. You'll misstep and hurt yourself or others. You'll bleed and bruise. You'll learn from your mistakes. All that being said, this doesn't mean you have to take unnecessary risks or blunder into known dangers. Here are some early and common pitfalls to avoid as you walk away from your religion.

Walking in Circles

Sometimes your surroundings look familiar because you're walking in circles. This is especially common when you're beginning a journey. Without accustomed landmarks, it often takes several circuits to realize you're getting nowhere. Below is a list of some of the more common circular routes:

- Mourning the same loss again and again. There were real losses in leaving your religion. Returning repeatedly to those losses is like leaving the church to hang out in the graveyard.
- Circling home. Living on the fringes of your religious community is common in the beginning. Staying there isn't. A prolonged need to revisit religious places and events could be avoiding the journey rather than staying connected.
- Debating your decision. Repeated arguments with the same person over your leaving are seldom productive. Either you have some heightened need for their validation or they have some need to control you. Neither need is healthy.
- Correcting perceptions. No matter what explanation you give for leaving, expect others to offer their own interpretations. Tracking and correcting these alternative explanations keeps you distracted. People will say what people say.

In each of these situations, you are allowing some fear – of loss, loneliness, rejection, or disapproval – to keep you from fully venturing out. Instead of walking away from your religion, you're walking around it. While this is a common early mistake, once you recognize it, you need to address it. If you cannot, you may be psychologically or emotionally stuck and need help overcoming these barriers to leaving. In a non-religious life, seeking counseling is a sign of self-awareness and self-care. Sometimes, in the beginning of a journey, you need someone to walk with you.

Seeking the Most Dangerous Paths

Another early error with potentially dire consequences is choosing the most dangerous or taboo path. Uncertain of what path to take, you select the path which differs the most from your previous religious path. If your religious tradition or community forbade certain activities or attitudes, you engage in…

- Broad and uninhibited sexual experimentation
- Over indulgence of taboo food, drink and other substances
- Immodesty and coarseness
- Greed and gross materialism
- Self-absorption

Or, if your religious tradition or community required certain practices, you forever avoid…

- Any type of daily meditation or quiet reflection
- Fasting or other acts of self-denial
- Generosity of time and money.
- Celebrating significant life milestones

Neither indiscriminate engagement in previously taboo activities or obsessive avoidance of all quasi-religious practices is a good approach. While you may decide many religious taboos or requirements have become meaningless to you, be cautious. Not every religious prohibition or prescription is nonsense, especially those with wider cultural support. If it makes no sense, don't obey it, but carefully unpack your motivation.

Ironically, choosing a path based on its deviation from your previously religious path is allowing your religious tradition to set your course. Doing what you were told you shouldn't takes little thought. Instead, take responsibility for your life and journey, carefully sorting through the values, opinions and practices of your religious tradition and creating your own criteria for choosing where to walk and what to do.

If you've made the mistake of rejecting all that was religiously tainted and choosing all that was previously taboo, don't be too hard on yourself. Many learn this lesson quickly and painfully. Indeed, this tendency on the part of those leaving religion fuels the religious claim that the non-religious become immoral. You may venture down a few paths you later regret. Fortunately, you won't make this mistake repeatedly. You will discover some paths aren't safe for anyone.

In many cases, while some of the trappings may differ, the lifestyle of a healthy non-religious person won't look markedly different than the lifestyle of a healthy religious life, nor should it. The good life is about good health, good relationships, good work and good play. Any path, religious or otherwise, that inhibits such goodness is to be avoided.

Fighting Rather Than Exploring

One of the ways of ignoring your fears and anxieties about venturing into the unknown is by distracting yourself. Sometimes people leave the religious mountain, find what they consider higher ground and raise fortifications. They do so expecting pursuit and attack by the religious. They choose to debate instead of reflect, to defend instead of explain and to fight instead of explore. This is especially tempting when your religious community was abusive or you're insecure. A good fight is better than flight.

If your experience of religion was abusive and controlling, you may tend toward this distraction. Faced with the uncertainties of becoming non-religious, it may be easier to fight the devil you know than risk the one you don't. You may have deep-seated fears about venturing alone into a potentially hostile world. Until you trust yourself and those around you, it will be very difficult to move anywhere.

If your religious experience was positive and you still want to fight, you may be the bully, avoiding your own insecurities by picking on others. Carefully examine your need to attack your religion. Why must religion be bad for you to move on? Why must religion be wrong for you to be right? Why must you attack a way of life that once brought you happiness and that is obviously still bringing others satisfaction?

Totalitarianism – a philosophic approach to life that adopts a rigid set of beliefs and attempts and imposes them on everyone else – isn't limited to religious fundamentalists. It can take equally ugly non-religious manifestations. If the imposition of your opinions remains your highest good, you have much in common with the very religious institutions you claim to despise.

This doesn't mean you shouldn't oppose attempts by religious people or institutions to impose their beliefs on you or others. You have a right and responsibility to voice your opinion, challenge the thinking of others and participate in ethical debate. Indeed, the freedom to defy institutional claims of divine authority is one of the rewards of becoming non-religious. What you want to avoid is becoming anti-religious instead of non-religious.

Ultimately, fighting instead of exploring means choosing to reframe your life as a battle instead of a journey. Your goal becomes philosophical victory instead of personal awareness and authenticity. You're defining yourself by what you've come to disdain rather than by what you hope and dream. In so doing, you risk forever facing the mountain with your back to the very country you hoped to explore.

Settling at the First Comfortable Spot

Another common mistake is looking for the familiar in the unfamiliar. Many people leave their religious community, its responsibilities, rituals and requirements and immediately seek out another community with similar responsibilities, rituals and requirements. Often, almost any community will do. They set up a permanent camp at the first comfortable spot they encounter after walking away from their religion.

This is a powerful temptation, especially when the initial journey away from religion can be solitary and frightening. After months of explaining and defending yourself, any place or group that accepts you can seem a welcome sanctuary. They will often share your disenchantment with your previous community, sympathize with your leaving and invite you to join them. Taking this path is sometimes a dead end, leading you to places where you quickly become as unhappy as you were with your religious community. Resist the urge to find a single place or group to meet your needs.

One of the common aims of a non-religious life is to seek and experience the wondrous and magical in a great variety of places and people. The religious approach often connects such experiences to a specific place – a sanctuary. Unfortunately, the need for a sanctuary exposes a deeply ingrained religious assumption – there is no goodness and safety in the world outside of religion. If you never abandon this assumption about the world, you'll never feel completely comfortable exploring that world. Instead of having one adventure after another, you will simply flee from sanctuary to sanctuary.

In walking away from religion, you are deciding there is happiness to be found almost anywhere. This is at the heart of being an explorer. You can willingly leave behind the peaceful meadow to explore beyond the next ridge. Even when you seek the familiar and comfortable, you search for it in a variety of places and with a variety of people.

When you encounter the familiar, you are connecting with far more than your religious roots. You are encountering that which your religion tried to contain. A beautiful sunset, a deep conversation, or an act of unexpected kindness may all evoke what you experienced in your religious life, but don't confuse such moments as a sign to stop exploring. A stroll through the forest may remind you of a moment in the temple, cathedral or mosque, but remember that people were strolling through forests long before anyone built a temple, cathedral or mosque.

Eventually, you may find a community with which you wish to settle down, though it may be for only a few seasons. Better yet, you may find a traveling troupe to join. Finding and creating community is important and meets a deep human need. The danger is not in seeking community, but in seeking it too soon and too permanently. If you can avoid this trap, you will save yourself the additional pain and struggle of leaving another place and people. You may also learn to meet some of your own needs.

Ignoring Your Legitimate Needs

One of the best defenses against settling in the first comfortable spot is acknowledging your legitimate needs for connection, intimacy and support. If you travel too long without companionship, food or rest, you are likely to make camp with anyone who can meet those needs. While taking responsibility for meeting your own needs is vital, it is dangerous to confuse personal autonomy with radical independence.

Initially, you will probably enjoy the solitude, space and freedom of walking away from your religion. There is a thrill in setting out on your own. Unfortunately, as mentioned earlier, you are ill equipped for such a journey. Your religious community has supplied many of your needs. If leaving your religious community was difficult, they probably did this well. Fairly soon, if these needs are not met, you will find your strength for the journey diminished.

Return to page 45 and review your list of the five benefits and advantages in being part of your religious community. These probably reflect legitimate needs in your life. Rewrite them as needs instead of benefits and advantages:

1.

2.

3.

4.

5.

While settling in the first comfortable spot isn't the proper strategy for meeting these needs, neither is ignoring them. If you don't take these needs seriously, you may meet them in inappropriate and unhealthy ways instead of carefully and intentionally meeting these needs through non-religious means. Later in this book, you'll be given help in doing this important work. For now, it is only necessary to acknowledge and accept you cannot make this journey while ignoring these needs.

Reflecting

Most people encounter some of these pitfalls when walking away from a religious tradition or community. Based on the previous descriptions, into which pits have you fallen? Briefly jot down personal examples:

- Walking In Circles

- Seeking the Most Dangerous Paths

- Fighting Instead of Exploring

- Settling at the First Comfortable Spot

- Ignoring Your Legitimate Needs

Circle the pitfall that has been the most troublesome. Reflect on why this was or has been the most problematic. What fear or anxiety did or does it represent for you? How can you avoid this same mistake in the future? When do you find yourself tempted to make this mistake again?

If you are early in your journey away from religion, reading these descriptions may help you avoid these traps. Unfortunately, if you're farther along in the journey, you may have made every one of these mistakes. If so, don't beat yourself up. Falling is a necessary part of learning to walk, even when you're walking away from your religion.

If you have recently left your religious community, you may be sitting in the bottom of one of these pits. If so, don't be embarrassed or discouraged. Get out, shake off the dirt, bandage your wounds and start walking again. One day soon you'll look back on these mistakes, laugh and celebrate how far you've come.

"Freedom is not worth having
if it does not include the freedom to make mistakes."

-Mahatma Gandhi

An Autobiography In Five Chapters

Chapter 1
I walk down the street.
There is a deep hole in the sidewalk.
I fall in.
I am lost...I am helpless.
It isn't my fault.
It takes forever to find a way out.

Chapter 2
I walk down the street.
There is a deep hole in the sidewalk.
I pretend that I don't see it.
I fall in again.
I can't believe I am in this same place.
But, it isn't my fault.
It still takes a long time to get out.

Chapter 3
I walk down the same street.
There is a deep hole in the sidewalk.
I *see* it is there.
I still fall in...it's a habit...but, my eyes are open.
I know where I am.
It is *my* fault.
I get out immediately.

Chapter 4
I walk down the same street.
There is a deep hole in the sidewalk.
I walk around it.

Chapter 5
I walk down another street.

-Portia Nelson

When you're part of a religious tradition,
you learn its vocabulary
and speak its language.

When you walk away from that tradition,
you discover you don't always have the words
to describe your new experiences and thoughts.

When you try,
you often resort to the
language, imagery and stories
you've always used.

Using religious language
to describe your new experiences and thoughts
can be confusing for you and others.

Even when people understand
what you're trying to say,
they will still hear your accent.

Learning to speak a non-religious language
with beauty and clarity
takes time and effort.

———————————

"A different language is a different vision of life."

-Federico Fellini

Learning a New Language

If you were raised in a religious tradition or community, you speak a religious language fluently. If you joined that tradition as an adult, you probably spent considerable time learning the nuances and accents of religious speech. You know its vocabulary, sentence structures and imagery. You understand its proverbs, metaphors and figures of speech. You understand the deeper meanings of the words and phrases

To the Muslim, words like "Islam" and "hajj" and "jihad" mean much more than their English translations of submission, pilgrimage and struggle. They represent assumptions about the purposes of life. To the Buddhist, "awakening the Buddha within" is far more than a figure of speech. To the Christian, being "saved" and "born again" come with a whole subtext and story line. Those who belong to a religious tradition can communicate entire worldviews in a single word or sentence.

When walking away from a religious tradition, you face an immediate challenge. If you value integrity and clear communication, you must wean yourself from your religious language with its unspoken assumptions while simultaneously learning a non-religious language that better represents the way you understand yourself and the world. As long as you rely on religious language, you will find it difficult to untangle yourself from the deeply embedded assumptions of your religious upbringing. You will also find it hard to be understood in non-religious settings.

Abandoning Religious Language

Losing a language doesn't happen overnight. It takes time and diligence to quit using religiously inspired words and phrases. You may find yourself slipping back easily and often into terminology that no longer adequately represents your understanding of the world. You'll also encounter situations where – if you don't use religious language – you won't have the words to describe an experience, feeling or idea.

In many ways, losing a religious language is easier than learning a non-religious one. Indeed, you've already begun this process. Some of your earliest religious dissatisfaction was the result of using words or phrases at odds with your new thinking. Now, as you walk away from religion, you hear yourself and others with new ears. You find yourself hearing religious language and asking, "Do I or they really mean that?" While they probably do, you obviously do not. Language that once tripped off your tongue, may suddenly get stuck in your throat.

Take a moment and write down any religious words or phrases that – when you recently heard or said them – made you uncomfortable.

As your opinions shift, your sensitivity to discrepancies and inconsistencies in your use of religious language will increase. You will be your best teacher and monitor. Friends and family – sometimes with mixed motives – will also point out when you use expressions at odds with your emerging non-religious worldview. Gradually, you will find yourself using religious language less and less often.

Though every religious tradition has its unique vocabulary, here are a few examples of widely shared religious words or phrases you may need to abandon:

- "Faith"
  You may still have faith in many things, but using this word implies a religious commitment. Being non-religious means no longer having a faith as religious folk understand it.

- "Holy"

  You may continue to believe in the magical, mystical and mysterious, but you probably ought to use those words. Holiness is often capitalized because it is so closely aligned with divinity and religion.

- "Sin"

  People certainly err, make mistakes, dysfunction and choose poorly. When this is called sin, you've involved a religious code and added judgment and punishment to the equation.

- "Blasphemy"

  This is what religious people will call much of what is written in this book. From here on, you'll have to give a more thoughtful response to words that offend you.

- "Heresy"

  This is what religious people call ideas they find upsetting. While the original Greek word simply meant "thinking differently," it is probably unwise to claim an identity as a heretic. In some places in the world, religions still murder heretics.

- "Evil"

  Like sin, evil presumes someone is in the position to judge and condemn. While naming people and actions as evil is a common religious practice, it is one best abandoned by the non-religious.

- "Jihad" or "Crusade"

  This is what usually happens after a religion identifies people or actions as evil. Whether you use this word or not, make certain you don't make a crusade of your non-religious opinions.

- "You're in my prayers."

  Telling someone they're in your prayers implies you pray. It also suggests a God who answers prayer. If you don't pray any longer, don't lie about it. Telling them that you're thinking about them can be equally kind.

- "Everything happens for a reason."
  In a religious framework, where God is thought to pull the strings, this may make sense. In a non-religious world, it's probably nonsense. Learning to be comfortable with the ambiguous and the random is key to becoming non-religious.

While this list is hardly exhaustive, it should give you a sampling of the kinds of words and phrases you may need to reevaluate. In general, you should avoid words or phrases that rely exclusively or heavily on religious assumptions. You may attempt to redefine or reclaim a word or phrase, but do so knowing most hearers will not share your revised definition. They will assume you intend the religious meaning. As with anyone learning a different language, mixing words from two languages should probably be a temporary necessity and not a permanent practice.

For a time, you may speak both languages, able to hear and understand the very different words and phrases religious and non-religious people use to describe the same ideas or events. You may even be called on to translate or interpret for others. As you use and hear religious language less and less, you may eventually find religious language odd or foreign. Indeed, some of it may even become incomprehensible. This is usually an indication you've begun to speak and think in another language.

Learning Non-Religious Language

If your ultimate goal is to communicate your understanding of yourself and of the world as clearly as possible, you will need to gradually replace religious words and phrases with non-religious ones. Though challenging, this can become great fun. It is an opportunity to explore a whole new set of words and phrases, some of which you may have once thought off limits. Long before you're fluent in this new language, you'll discover words or phrases you enjoy saying.

Becoming fluent in any language takes time. Be patient. First, you'll learn a few key phrases. Then you'll expand your vocabulary of nouns and verbs. Eventually, sentences and paragraphs will come together. Your goal is not to simply speak the language, but to think in it, to understand the complexities and beauty of its underlying assumptions. Don't worry about your initial clumsiness with non-religious language. Don't allow your inability to speak fluently keep you from speaking at all. The only way to learn a new language is to use it.

When you begin learning a language, you often begin with a few key phrases. Here are a few examples of phrases you may find helpful as you begin speaking non-religious language:

- "That doesn't work for me."
This may be the first non-religious phrase you need to learn. In a religious context, whether something works for you is irrelevant. If the religion commands, you are to believe and obey. When you try to explain your shifting thoughts, you may initially explain it with religious phrases like "I'm feeling led" or "I've come to believe." Using religious language to explain becoming non-religious doesn't work. It also invites debate over your leadings and beliefs. Until you learn more complex non-religious language, saying "that doesn't work for me" is the best option for explaining your disbelief.

- "What is your evidence for that?"
The demand for evidence is another significant phrase. In a religious context, beliefs based on faith or revelation are sufficient. In the non-religious world, conclusions require evidence. The more important the conclusion, the more significant the evidence should be. As you walk away from your religion and explore the world, you will meet people with many divergent ideas and opinions. They will point you in various directions. Asking them for their evidence will help you avoid dead ends and unnecessary detours.

- "Even if God exists…" or "Even if God doesn't exist…"
These disclaimers are not in the religious lexicon. Even if you continue to believe in God, they should probably be in yours. They serve two purposes. They quickly identify you as a non-religious person and they proclaim your willingness to live responsibly in a non-religious world. "Even if God exists, I think I should act in this way" or "Even if God doesn't exist, I think I should act in that way" equally emphasize your willingness to take responsibility for your choices and actions.

- "I'm non-religious"

Religion supplies a quick and easy identifier – Christian, Muslim, Jew, Buddhist. When you walk away from religion, you need new language to describe yourself. If you don't identify yourself, others will. Many adopt the term spiritual. Unfortunately, this is using a religious word to explain a non-religious status. While there are a variety of options, initially you may want to simply identify as non-religious. This placeholder provides an identifier until you've developed non-religious words that better describe your specific journey.

Words are important. Finding the best words to describe what you experience, think and conclude is one of the ways you explore your world. In learning a different language, you often begin with key nouns – words that describe specific objects or ideas. While these words may sometimes be similar in different languages, they can also be different and distinct. Below are two lists. The first column is of nouns that are strongly associated with religion. The second is of potential non-religious equivalents:

Religious	**Non-Religious**
God/Allah	Universe, Connection
Creation	World
Sin	Mistake, Poor decision
Prayer	Meditation
Heaven/Hell	Afterlife
Faith	Philosophy
Belief	Thought, opinion, idea
Heresy	Different thought, opinion, or idea
Certainty	Probability
Revelation	Reflection
Blessing	Good fortune
Fellowship	Party

Miracle	Wonder
Idol	Obsession
Spirit	Mystery
Ministry	Service
Bible/Quran/Torah	Religious writing
Commandment	Religious code
Heathen/Pagan/Infidel	Non-religious

You'll notice in each of these instances the religious word and the non-religious word – while intending to describe the same object or idea – reflect very different assumptions. Choosing to use one word over the other reveals your worldview. As you depart from religious circles, you will hear more nouns from the second column and less from the first. Eventually, the religious nouns – though you understand their meaning – will sound stilted.

Verbs are a little trickier. Both religious and non-religious folk use many of the same verbs. Though some verbs have developed strong religious undertones, completely avoiding them is probably impossible. As a non-religious person, it is enough to be aware of the religious uses of these words. Verbs with varying religious baggage include:

- Reveal, ordain, sanctify, bless, atone, baptize, crucify, sacrifice, convict, repent, resurrect, glorify, blaspheme, fornicate, tempt, crusade, deny, anoint, confess, redeem, save, pray, worship, adore, minister, praise, revive, tolerate, judge, submit and believe.

You may decide to quit using some of these verbs completely. You may use others more cautiously, always aware of their religious echo. Again, becoming aware of the assumptions behind your choice of words is the goal. Do the words you use best represent the way you understand the world?

As a non-religious person you may find these verbs more common and useful as you describe your experience and actions:

- Evolve, critique, doubt, speculate, disbelieve, question, adapt, explore, inquire, evaluate, imagine, risk, reflect, meditate, examine, experiment, enjoy, analyze, balance, choose, theorize, wonder, ponder, marvel and think.

Many of these verbs involve acts of decision making. Rather than implying God will act, intervene or influence, they assume you are personally responsible for creating and engaging. They illustrate many of the underlying assumptions of a non-religious life.

Becoming Fluent

Fluency is more than being able to communicate in a language. It is appreciating and enjoying the complexities and beauty of the words and phrases. Initially, replacing religious language with non-religious speech will be a sometimes frustrating and exhausting chore. You'll slip back and forth between the two. You'll make mistakes. You'll miscommunicate.

Be patient. Eventually, the new words will begin to flow. You will discover yourself not only using these new words, but developing a deeper understanding of the assumptions behind them. Non-religious language has its own power and beauty. There are words you seldom used while religious that will suddenly become common and vibrant.

For example, the phrase "I don't know" is rare in religious speech. Religions are quick to supply answers to nearly every question. The religious are encouraged to offer these answers to others, asked or unasked. When faced with difficult questions about human suffering, destiny and meaning, the religious seldom respond with "I don't know." To do so is to acknowledge ambiguity, uncertainty and doubt.

As a non-religious person, you should learn to use this phrase often. Saying you don't know is not an admission of defeat and a reason to despair. As an explorer of the world, acknowledging what you do not know is a good starting point. You are free to look anywhere and everywhere for possible answers and explanations. Accepting that there is much you'll never know takes away the pressure of quickly ending uncertainty. You journey expecting – if you are courageous, open and curious – some mysteries will be solved, others will be less frightening and still others will remain forever unknown. You just don't know which mysteries will be which.

This is the beauty of non-religious language. It values – rather than fears - the ambiguous, the uncertain and the unknown. It is more fluid, willing to utilize a variety of words to name a single experience, event or object. It is more personal, allowing each person their unique description of what they see, hear and feel. Since no two paths will be exactly alike, no two narratives should use exactly the same words.

For these reasons, many non-religious phrases begin with "I think." This phrase claims personal responsibility for whatever descriptions of the world that follow. In religious speech, the more common beginning is "I believe." Though "think" and "believe" are often used interchangeably, they are not the same. To believe is to trust, have faith in, accept as true and be certain of. In using it at the beginning of any sentence, you are often claiming the description of someone else about the world. Religions create and value believers.

This is not to suggest religious people do not think or the non-religious are immune from beliefs. The problem is that believing has become the predominant verb for religion. It so governs that in some religious circles thinking is discouraged and intellectual inquiry mocked. When the religious do think, they are often discouraged from thinking about a whole range of questions and topics. Some thoughts are blasphemous, heretical and taboo.

Thinkers ignore such things. They consider all they encounter, ponder the possibilities, reflect on their own motives and prejudices, theorize about what might be and experiment. The words they utter carry no universal authority or divine inspiration. They must be judged on their merits, trusted only if they resonate. When thoughts prove inadequate, they can choose to think differently. Changing an opinion is not nearly as ominous as changing a belief.

Your quick and easy use of phrases like "I don't know" and "I think" are signs you are not simply learning a new language. You are thinking differently. Changes in your pattern of speech indicate a profound shift in how you understand yourself and the world. As you become more comfortable as a non-religious person, your words, thoughts and actions will eventually harmonize. The language you use to describe the world will fit your experience of it. Though a religious accent may always remain, you will speak the language of your head and your heart.

"Change your language and you change your thoughts."

-Karl Albrecht

When you first become non-religious,
your life may outwardly look the same
as it did when you were religious.

For some, this is because your religious identity
was never your primary identity.
If you seldom identified publicly as religious,
becoming non-religious is more of a personal shift
than a public one.

For those from evangelical or cultural religious traditions,
or those previously in religious leadership,
you probably proudly and publicly identified
as religious for many years.

People know you've abandoned beliefs,
quit attending religious services,
or left your religious community.

Whether your departure from religion
was private or public,
you will eventually need
to identify as a non-religious person,
to build openly non-religious relationships
and eliminate religious vestiges.

There comes a moment in every journey
when you must identify yourself by where you live
and not by where you came from.

Clarifying Your Identity

While any change in identity is potentially tricky, those that require you to redefine yourself radically take time and finesse. The stronger your identity as a religious person, the more complicated altering your identity can be. The more exclusive your religious community, the more difficult it will be to visit new places and trust new people. The longer you existed as a religious person, the more time it will probably take to free yourself of all the baggage you've collected along the way.

How you left your religious community can aid or inhibit your adoption of a new identity. If your departure was fairly public, most people will learn of your status via the grapevine. Neither you nor they can pretend nothing has changed. If you left more gradually and quietly, many may still assume you're religious. Regardless, as you become more comfortable in your non-religious skin, you will have occasions and opportunities to identify yourself as a non-religious person.

Initially, like with religious and non-religious language, you may spend months or even years living in two worlds. As you struggle with your beliefs, you also struggle with your identity. You may claim a religious or non-religious identity dependent on your given setting, audience, or feelings at the time. If so, this is normal, especially when you're living in the shadow of the mountain. However, once you walk away from the mountain, identifying yourself by continually pointing back toward it becomes less and less authentic. There comes a day when you are no longer a mountain dweller. You need another name for yourself.

Identifying yourself as non-religious – or by any other term you find authentic – helps you and others understand how you think about the world. It clarifies your values and allegiances when you initiate or deepen a relationship with someone. Identifying yourself as non-religious can force you to finally clean house and remove the vestiges of the religious identity you no longer claim.

Choosing a Public Identity

Assuming you've told the most significant people in your life about becoming non-religious, you still face the task of developing a non-religious identity. Though this book has – and will continue to use – non-religious as an identifier, it simply serves as a placeholder until you determine what works best for you.

The following list includes some of the most common identifiers used by people after they leave a religion. They are arranged in three categories, each with their advantages or disadvantages. As you read the terms, cross out those you find problematic and circle those you find attractive.

- Reactive Identifiers

  These terms clearly say what you are not, but may not adequately communicate what you now think or value.

  - Non-religious

  - Non-believer

  - Recovering Christian, Muslim, Jew, Buddhist, etc.

  - Ex-Christian, ex-Muslim, ex-Jew, ex-Buddhist, etc.

  - Agnostic

  - Atheist

  - Skeptic

- Semi-Religious Identifiers

  These terms may communicate what you think or value, but may be confused as religious.

  - Spiritual or Spiritualist

  - Mystical or Mystic

  - Seeker

- Heretic

- Pagan

- **Proactive Identifiers**

  These terms are more descriptive of a new approach, but may require considerable explanation when used.

  - Humanist

  - Secular or Secular Humanist

  - Free Thinker

  - Naturalist

  - Rationalist

This is not an exhaustive list. You may use all these identifiers or none of them. You may use different identities depending on the situation and your audience. You may begin using one of these and gradually move to another. What you cannot do is think your identity is irrelevant. Whether you're filling out a survey, admitted to a hospital, talking with an acquaintance, going out on a date, or seeking political office, you will probably be asked to identify yourself in relationship to religion. How you choose to respond – even if you refuse to identify yourself – will determine how you are seen or understood.

Indeed, choosing not to identify yourself is giving away some of your autonomy. When you don't name yourself, others will name you. Even when you do claim an identity, some will dislike, discount or ignore it, preferring to name you something comfortable for them. Based on your history, some will insist on identifying you as what you were. If you resist this, they may call you an atheist whether your find this descriptive or comfortable.

Others will conclude your fluid identity is a sign of indecisiveness or confusion rather than honest exploration. They may pat your hand

and assure you – that once this identity crisis is over – you'll see the light and return to the fold. Truth be told, you may never settle on one identity. You may decide no single identity will ever again adequately describe who you are.

These external pressures are all good reasons to choose a new identity, but the best reason is far more compelling. In naming yourself, you do something central to being non-religious – you take responsibility for your life. You announce your willingness to leave the old behind, embrace the ambiguity of the present and explore what ultimately describes you and your vision of the world most accurately. Like the Native American approach to naming children, you have the opportunity to fit your name to your experience or aspirations. Whatever you choose, it will belong to you.

Once you publicly claim and utilize an identity, it becomes much easier to navigate in a world where so many want to tell you who you are and what you should think. It also becomes easier to explore new places and meet new people. When they ask who you are, you can tell them.

Non-Religious Relationships in Non-Religious Places

As a religious person, there were places you weren't to go and people you weren't to engage. The first time you violate one of those taboos can feel odd, exciting, confusing and freeing – all at the same time. For some, after years of denying or pretending you are something you are not, finding places where you can be yourself can be wonderful.

Unfortunately, it isn't always easy to find such places and people, especially since you often have to overcome past fears and inhibitions. Though flaunting your identity as a non-religious person in every public setting or with perfect strangers isn't healthy, avoiding places and people your religious tradition prohibited is equally unnecessary. It either indicates unresolved fears about leaving your religion or anxieties about this unfamiliar world you're exploring.

Below is a list of some of the places and people that – while you were religious – you may have never visited or engaged. Circle those that provoke any fear or anxiety.

Places	People
A bar	Atheists
A X-rated movie	Gays or Lesbians
A philosophy class	People of another religion
A New Age bookstore	Abortionists
A tattoo shop	Polygamists
A casino	People of another race
A lingerie shop	Astrologists
A therapist's office	Communists
A gun shop	Feminists
An abortion clinic	Liberals
A Masonic lodge	Massage therapists
A Head Shop	Non-Religious people

This is not intended as a list of places you should visit or people you should engage. As a non-religious person, you may have good reason for avoiding some of these places and people. The issue, as you review the places and people you circled, is whether you are avoiding them because of personal reasons or because of religious taboos and prejudices. If you circled nothing, you are bringing little baggage from your religious upbringing. If you circled many, you have a tougher challenge ahead. Regardless, as a previously religious person, whenever you find yourself hesitant to visit a place or engage with a person, it may be worth examining your reasoning.

As a non-religious person, you are free to go wherever and to associate with whomever you choose. As in any journey, there are paths with more risk than others and even some where only the foolhardy tread. Choosing destinations simply because your religion declared them off limits isn't wise, but there may be places your religion cursed that could bring you satisfaction and joy. As for avoiding certain people, it's helpful to remember you are now on the taboo list of most religions.

Becoming non-religious is the opportunity to discover all the richness of humanity, with its wide spectrum of personalities and approaches to life. If you identify yourself as non-religious in casual conversations, you may be surprised how many people are hungry to talk about their opinions, thoughts and ideas without religious constraints. Sometimes, when you identify as non-religious, others will find the courage to share their own identities. This reluctance on the part of many to openly identify as non-religious demonstrates the continued power of religion in our culture. It isn't easy for non-religious people to recognize each other in public.

It is difficult, but not impossible. Ironically, one trick for identifying other non-religious people occurs whenever you are in a public setting where there is a prayer. Instead of bowing your head and closing your eyes – a habit of nearly every religious person – look around the room. When you do so, you will find a few others who are also unbowed and looking around. Often, if you make eye contact, you realize you've identified another non-religious person.

With time, you will become aware of other subtle indications people are non-religious. You will notice the nouns and verbs they use or don't use. You'll note the places they mention visiting or people they count as friends. You'll recognize the absence of the many vestiges and habits of the religious life. Just as with religious affiliation, once you learn what to look for, it will become easier and easier to identify the non-religious. In so doing, you'll also become more aware of the mixed signals you may be sending about your identity.

Eliminating Religious Vestiges and Habits

When you were religious, you were given or obtained many symbols of your religious affiliation. You developed many religious habits and practices. When you become non-religious, you don't immediately divest yourself of all of these symbols. Old habits and practices linger, even when you find them embarrassing or irritating.

The elimination of religious vestiges and habits is an important step in identifying as a non-religious person. Resistance to this personal housecleaning could be an indication of continued denial, grief or even shame. You may be keeping these familiar tokens or continuing the habitual practices of your previous identity to lighten your pain or the pain of others. Unfortunately, when you do so, you give a false impression. You may actually prolong the pain. Eventually, you will need to sit down and intentionally sort through the possessions and habits of your life.

For some, this will seem a daunting challenge, almost a reason to return to the faith. Fortunately, this personal housecleaning need not be immediate or hasty. Throwing out every object with any religious connection is a little like discarding every possession you shared with an ex-spouse. As satisfying as that can be, you may realize later than some of those objects still had value. The best process is gradual and thoughtful.

Take your time and carefully consider what objects have nostalgic and historic value rather than religious power. Examine your habits and practices to differentiate between what has personal meaning and utility and what remains a religious compulsion. Some objects and habits will need to go quickly, others will take longer to abandon and some will become treasured reminders of from where you've come. The objects and habits one non-religious person keeps will not be the same as another non-religious person, nor should they be.

There is perhaps one exception. Non-religious persons should probably request their removal from membership in their religious community. For some, this decision will be made for you. Once you quit attending services or meeting other obligations, you will be quickly removed from membership. For most, your religious community is like Hotel California – you can check out any time you like, but you can never leave. The membership rolls of most religious groups are full of the names of people who now consider themselves non-religious. It would probably be better for you and for your former religious community if you were both honest about your identity.

Ending an important relationship is difficult, but it is less difficult when done well. Slipping out the back door, allowing others to hear of your leaving through the grapevine is a poor way to end a relationship. Once you're ready to publicly identify as a non-religious person, it is an act of respect to write your former religious community a short note requesting your removal from membership.

Once you formally end your membership in your religious community, you are ready for the more time consuming work of taking personal inventory of your possessions and practices to determine what to discard and what to keep. The following two lists – one of objects and the other of habits – should help you begin to sort through the remaining vestiges of your religious life. As you review the first list, you may want indicate what you wish to trash (T), further consider (C), or keep (K). Some may not apply to you..

Religious Symbols and Objects Inventory

T C K   Religious painting and art hanging in your home

T C K   Religiously themed bumper stickers or signs

T C K   Clothing with religious logos or symbols

T C K   Your religion's holy writings

T C K   Other religious books and devotional literature

T C K   Religiously themed music

T C K   Religious holiday symbols and paraphernalia

T C K   Religious certificates and mementos

135

T	C	K	Religious jewelry, necklaces and rings
T	C	K	Prayer rugs, prayer beads and rosaries
T	C	K	Religious headwear/head coverings
T	C	K	Religious tokens, icons and medals
T	C	K	Kosher food
T	C	K	Religious undergarments
T	C	K	Religious phylacteries

Again, this is not an exhaustive list. Every religious tradition and community imbues different objects with meaning. The question for you is whether keeping these objects confuse you or others about your identity. What do the objects you own and display say about who you are and what you think?

Fortunately, only family and close friends may see many of these objects. More difficult to ignore are those habits you practice more publicly and which may be interpreted as religiously motivated. In the following list, indicate those habits and practices you either need to end (E), further consider (C), or keep (K). Again, some may not apply to you.

<u>Religious Habits and Practices Inventory</u>

E	C	K	Cutting your hair in a certain manner
E	C	K	Bowing your head during prayer
E	C	K	Table blessings
E	C	K	Religious greetings and farewells
E	C	K	Quoting religious verses or writings
E	C	K	Tithing or almsgiving
E	C	K	Daily prayer or reflective reading

E	C	K	Growing or shaving facial hair
E	C	K	Having your son circumcised
E	C	K	Getting married or buried in a religious setting
E	C	K	Baptizing or dedicating infants
E	C	K	Participating in your religion's coming of age ritual
E	C	K	Praying for the sick
E	C	K	Avoiding certain foods and drinks
E	C	K	Addressing people by using religious titles/terms

This is merely a sampling of the vast number of religious habits and practices you may engage in. Some of them are so ingrained and unconscious you won't initially realize they are religiously motivated. Long after you identify as non-religious, you will still occasionally realize something you're doing has religious overtones or influences. Then, as now, you'll need to determine if this practice is detrimental or confusing to you or others. Changing all your habits may be necessary, especially if you need to make a clean sweep, but you will probably end some and continue others.

Even when you decide to continue certain practices, you may keep the form, but redefine the purpose and meaning. For example, you may continue spending time each morning quietly meditating or reflecting. What was once a religious habit may become a helpful and satisfying non-religious practice. Or you may choose to have your son circumcised as a health decision rather than a religious ceremony. While you should do what makes sense to you, be aware it can be confusing for friends and family still in your former religious community. You may have to help them understand your motivation.

There is one final set of habits that deserve special attention – the habits you develop around religious holidays. Often, these holidays are a mishmash of religious and cultural practices. Sorting through the holiday habits motivated by your religious history and those more connected to a cultural or family history can be tricky. Eliminating

Christmas or Hanukah, or no longer participating in Ramadan may not be necessary, especially if your celebration of them was previously more a matter of nostalgia or cultural unity than religious observance.

Your task, as with objects or habits, is determining what will continue to confuse you or others. If you understood the holiday as an opportunity to connect with people you love, you may change very little about how you participate. On the other hand, if you were deeply invested in the religious meaning of the holiday, you may disconnect from some holiday trappings, events and practices. Fortunately, most religious holidays have become cultural events as well. You can often participate in parts of the holiday without necessarily implying you find the religious connection valid or important.

You may also emphasize different holidays, those with less or no religious connection. You may create new gatherings and celebrations. Kwanzaa is an example of a holiday created by those who wanted to celebrate their unique African history and values. As a non-religious person, you may choose to honor and celebrate ideas, moments or people that represent your view of the world. Many non-religious people appreciate and observe Earth Day.

No matter how you handle holidays, remember others will continue to find those holidays meaningful and value your presence. Just because the party isn't for you doesn't mean you can't attend. Focus on the relationships you treasure rather than the rituals you don't.

A Final Word

At the beginning of this section of the book, leaving your religion was described as walking away from a mountain. Redefining your public persona is what you do when you finally grow tired of being identified as a mountain dweller. When people ask who you are, you stop pointing back to the haze-obscured peaks of a place you no longer live. You identify yourself as someone who is either visiting their community or who is traveling their path.

No longer are you afraid of exploring new places or encountering different people. You've walked taboo paths and discovered some of the people you were warned to avoid make good friends. Some of them are people who once lived on the mountain as well, but many know you only as you are now. They may hear your accent, notice a few peculiar possessions and an occasional odd habit, but they find you as interesting and original as you find them.

For the first time since you left the mountain, you may feel completely free. This non-religious life that once frightened you has begun to feel comfortable and satisfying. What you once saw as risky seems interesting and fun. The rewards are finally outnumbering the losses. You are no longer becoming non-religious. You are non-religious. The next challenge is living this approach to life with integrity and authenticity.

"No one man can, for any considerable time, wear one face to himself, and another to the multitude, without finally getting bewildered as to which is the true one."

-Nathaniel Hawthorne

Calling yourself non-religious
and being non-religious are not the same thing.

As with any new identity,
you will probably claim the title before you acquire
the knowledge, competency and comfort
that come with time and experience.

Non-religious people meet their needs for
community and intimacy,
routine and ritual,
principled decision making,
inspiration, introspection and service
with ease and enjoyment.

You may not be there,
but you can be.

You can find and create community,
settle into new routines,
develop different rituals,
hone your principles,
find new inspiration,
learn to reflect,
and serve the world in fulfilling ways.

You can become a non-religious person
with a non-religious lifestyle.

Developing a Non-Religious Lifestyle

Up until now, much of this book has been about your desire and struggle for authenticity. A lack of authenticity was probably at the root of your dissatisfaction with your religion. A desire to become authentic likely spurred your eventual decision to leave. In the very act of walking away, you met this need for authenticity.

Unfortunately, in leaving your religious community, you've discovered authenticity was not your only need. Even at the end, your religious tradition and community may have meet significant needs – some of which are not now being met, or not being met as fully as you would like. You may still mourn those losses or miss those resources. This section of the book offers various tools and suggestions for meeting legitimate needs in non-religious ways, for developing a non-religious lifestyle.

It does not, however, provide a one-for-one replacement for your religious community and tradition. If you've been waiting for direction on a specific group to join, habits to practice, rituals to adopt, principles to uphold, heroes to claim, thoughts to think and acts to do, you may be disappointed. There is no non-religious map with a non-religious path to a non-religious destination. Unlike a religious lifestyle, where much of how you thought and acted was prescribed and packaged, a non-religious lifestyle is hard to describe or define. Once you leave the mountain, there are hundreds of paths with thousands of forks. You need a compass rather than a map because you can go in any direction.

The characteristics of a non-religious lifestyle are different than those of the religious lifestyle and understanding this new way of thinking is critical. You can drag the mountain behind you. You can leave a religious tradition or community and still live a largely religious lifestyle. You can make a religion out of your non-religiosity. It is important, as you seek to meet any unmet needs, to review and remember some of the most distinctive characteristics of a non-religious lifestyle.

Choosing Camping Sites and Companions

A non-religious lifestyle has no pre-determined destination or schedule. It's a stroll through the woods, not a marathon. As you explore, there should be moments of recreation, reflection and rest. You should walk with your head up, aware of the beautiful places and interesting people all around you. Often, you may find yourself setting up your tent near some gentle stream, quiet meadow or breathtaking vista. At other times, you'll meet people with whom you'd like to share a fire and shoot the breeze. Enjoy these moments..

In choosing when to stop, remove your backpack and set up camp, ask these questions:

> *What do I find satisfying and interesting about this approach, place or people? Why do I think one or more of my needs might be met? What do I find attractive or inspiring?*

Often, you will realize you're attracted to approaches, places or people that remind you of home, of the religious tradition or community you left. This is understandable and often harmless. As long as you're not seeking to replicate your religious past, meeting your needs in similar ways can be very satisfying. Make certain you don't limit your camping sites or companions to what feels familiar.

Explore the unknown. Don't avoid approaches, places and people because they are unlike what you've experienced and seen before. Instead, look for what intrigues or inspires, what stretches your imagination and takes your breath away. As a former mountain dweller, don't miss the grandeur of a canyon or the vastness of the sea. If you encounter people cooking something you've never smelled and sleeping in a yurt, explore how they meet their needs. Taste. Touch. Experiment. You may find your needs met in surprising ways.

Expecting To Pull Up Stakes

A non-religious lifestyle tempers its expectations. Wherever you set up camp, remember no single approach, place or people can forever meet all of your needs. Don't expect what is satisfying and interesting today to be equally satisfactory in a few months or years. If you create this expectation for whatever new approach, place or people you find, you are setting yourself up for the same painful disenchantment and disengagement you experienced in leaving your religion. Monitor your happiness and satisfaction, continually seeking to live as authentically as you're able.

Periodically, ask yourself these questions:

> *Is this approach, place or people still meeting one or more of my needs? Am I expecting it or them to meet too many needs? Am I expecting to always be satisfied and happy? Should I adjust my expectations or do I explore elsewhere?*

In asking these questions, you may discover you've become lazy and comfortable. If the new approach, place or people was attractive because of its familiarity, you may be slipping back into a religious mindset and expected this approach, place or people to permanently meet all your needs. Your unhappiness may be a sign of unrealistic expectations rather than another crisis.

A non-religious lifestyle is not a quest for paradise. Not every day will be satisfying and happy. No matter how beautiful the place you camp, don't expect it to never rain. Don't pull up stakes the first time an approach becomes difficult, a place becomes dreary or people become irritating. Don't confuse an authentic life with a fantasy life free of struggles and challenges.

Sometimes your happiness and satisfaction will be restored simply by adjusting your expectations. However, if this doesn't work, you may need to explore elsewhere. Remember, this is not an indictment of that approach, place or the people who still find that approach or place satisfying. As with your religion, you're leaving because what once met your needs no longer works. This usually has less to do with the approach, place, or people and more to do with what is happening in you.

Campsites are temporary. No matter how long you pitch your tent in a specific place, there may be a morning when you awake to that familiar feeling of deep dissatisfaction. Don't panic. You've done this before. It is not the end of the world. It's just the beginning of the next part of your adventure. Celebrate all that was good, say your good-byes to those you've been camping with and start hiking again.

For the reasons above, don't promise too much. One of the reasons it was difficult for you and others when you left your religion was because you probably vowed at some point to be faithful forever. Don't replace that vow with another. Make certain you and those with whom you engage understand you're on a journey.

The commitments you make - and you should make commitments - should always be qualified by your commitment to authenticity and the personal happiness and satisfaction it brings. While you should never end a commitment to an approach, place, or people rashly, neither should you remain in any situation where you're once again living a life of pretense.

Trusting Your Own Compass

A non-religious lifestyle is a journey within as much as a journey in the world. Early in your travels, accustomed to living your life in the company of others, walking alone can be uncomfortable. Looking for people with whom to travel or set up camp is understandable. However, as you become more at ease with the journey, there should come a time when you no longer assume the answer is always in a different approach, place or people. What you need may be within you.

Whenever you find yourself dissatisfied or unhappy, ask yourself these questions:

> *Do I really need a different approach, place or people to meet this need? Why am I looking outside myself? How can I meet this need? Can I create - rather than seek - something fulfilling?*

One of the most tenacious religious messages is that you are sinful, broken, inadequate and insufficient, that only with the aid of God or God's earthly servants do you have any hope of feeling worthy and finding happiness. Many who walk away from religion do so unaware they still carry this message in their backpack. If you continually look outside yourself for some approach, place or people to meet a specific need, you may be insecure about meeting your own needs.

This is a delicate distinction. There is nothing inherently wrong in seeking what has worked for others, or visiting places meaningful to many, or consulting with those who've traveled more widely. Often, in experimenting with various approaches, exploring different places or engaging diverse people, you are legitimately taking responsibility for your life. Sometimes, however, you are giving that responsibility away.

A non-religious lifestyle takes full responsibility for the task of meeting personal needs. As you walk away from religion, there should be more occasions when you hike and camp alone, when you test your capacity for meeting your own needs. Trusting your internal compass, you determine your dreams and desires and set off in that direction, not because others have walked or are walking that path, but because that is the direction you want to go.

In taking personal reasonability, you hope to eliminate the voids, vulnerabilities and inadequacies that made religion seem so attractive or necessary. You are learning to listen to the voices in your head and recognize which voice is yours. You are trusting that voice and what it tells you about yourself and the world.

In the pages that follow, there are many suggestions for meeting your needs. Try those that seem interesting. Ignore those that don't. If none resonate, don't despair. Sometimes you will find what you need. More often, your inability to find what you seek will inspire you to create it.

"We have to continually be jumping off cliffs
and developing our wings on the way down."

-Kurt Vonnegut

Finding and Creating Community

"You wanna be where you can see, our troubles are all the same.
You wanna be where everybody knows your name."

When you first left your religious community, you may have thought you were losing community forever. Suddenly separated from all it offered, you may have worried religion had a monopoly on community, or at least the supportive community you had enjoyed. Hopefully, you have already discovered this is false.

Society is rich with communities, gatherings of men and woman around mutual interests, concerns, beliefs and practices. The quote at the top of this page is from the theme song of a television show – *Cheers* – about a bar. Community – at its very heart – is the desire to be with people who understand your struggles and call you by name. While the thought of a bar as a credible community may seem farfetched to some, there are probably more people in bars on Saturday night than in churches on Sunday morning. Humans have an innate ability to create community often and nearly everywhere.

Once you understand this, you can understand the experience of leaving a religious community differently. You have not lost community. You've merely lost community in a single place and package. Religious communities are the social, emotional and psychological Sam's Clubs of the world. If you pay your membership dues, all your needs are met under one roof.

As a non-religious person, you are cutting up your membership card and exploring in small shops and boutiques for what you once found in a single place. Hopefully, this change of approach is exciting. You can seek community wherever you like.

Community is everywhere. You are already part of many communities. You belong to a country, a state, a town, a neighborhood and a family. You may also belong to professions, clubs, associations, interest groups, political parties and fraternities. As you leave a religious community, it is helpful to identify the other communities to which you belong. List four of your present communities and the key needs they meet in your life:

Communities   Needs Met

1.

2.

3.

4.

Now list four of significant needs your religious community met:

1.

2.

3.

4.

Examine these two lists. What are the needs your religious community met that are being or could be met by another of your communities? What are the gaps between what your religious community provided and what you're experiencing outside that community? Hopefully, in doing this exercise, you are more aware of your present resources. There also may be significant gaps. You will need to find or create ways to meet these needs.

In seeking new community, remember the assumptions of a non-religious lifestyle. Choose your campsites and companions wisely. Don't simply look for communities that remind you of your religious community. Think about some group of people who inspire or interest you. How do you connect with that group of people, to gather or work with them?

Explore various communities, ever cautious of committing too fully or expecting too much. Avoid communities that promise to meet all of your needs or ask for your sole allegiance. You've done that before and know the pitfalls. Look for different communities to meet different needs.

Consider creating what you cannot find. Remember, a non-religious life is about taking personal responsibility for your life. While visiting and experimenting with different communities is worthwhile, even more empowering is creating your own community. Who are the kind of people you'd enjoy being with? What would you discuss or do with them? How would you identify and recognize such people? How would you gather them?

One sign of independence is when you no longer make camp only where others are already camping. Find a beautiful place and pitch your tent. If others share your opinion of that place, let them join you. If they do so, create the community you desire. If no one joins you, enjoy that place anyway.

Don't confuse community with proximity. As you learned toward the end of your religious life, you can surround yourself with people and still feel different and alone. In a non-religious life, sometimes you discover what you really need is intimacy. Where you once sought the crowd and its validation, you may now seek a few kindred minds and hearts, individuals who really understand how you think and what you value.

If the prospect of creating community feels exhausting, consider the possibility that you may not need the same type or level of community as you once did. This may have even been part of your disenchantment with your religious community. You may be ready to journey with a few close friends, or even alone.

"I often warn people: "Somewhere along the way, someone is going to tell you, 'There is no "I" in team.' What you should tell them is, 'Maybe not. But there is an "I" in independence, individuality and integrity.""

-George Carlin

Adapting and Developing Routines and Rituals

Religions are good at creating life sustaining routines and life affirming rituals. At the end of your religious life, though some of these religious routines and rituals had probably lost much of their usefulness and power, there were probably others you were reluctant to abandon.

For some, the most difficult loss is the weekly religious services you attended. These services – by their very design - may have met a variety of your needs. In the beginning of your religious life, those services may have been a time to be with family, connect with friends, be entertained, study, think, be inspired, meditate, reflect and hear of ways you could support others in your religious community and around the world. You may have looked forward all week to those gatherings.

Obviously, toward the end of your religious life, your experience of those religious services probably changed. You may have come to dread attending. You probably found little of the content entertaining, thought provoking or inspiring. Religious services met fewer and fewer of your needs. In the end, you probably tolerated irritation or boredom in order to remain connected to friends and family. In many cases, what you really miss is that connectivity and not the content of the services.

Remember, that toward the end, your religious services weren't meeting many of your needs. You were already seeking elsewhere for entertainment, introspection, inspiration and service opportunities. You were already developing alternative routines and practices. Indeed, part of the reason you finally left may have been so you could focus your energies and attention on what was working instead of what wasn't. The day you quit attending religious services may have been a relief rather than a loss. Even if it wasn't, you can adapt and develop new routines.

A non-religious lifestyle does not require radically reordering your life. It can easily accommodate useful routines and redefine past rituals. As a non-religious person, how you order your year, month, week or day may remain remarkably unchanged. Much of the shift is in how you interpret what you're doing. Non-religious people value and celebrate important moments in life as often as religious people do. What differs is in how they understand the meaning of such occasions.

Examine the following list of common religious routines and rituals. Each is paired with a possible non-religious adaptation. Circle adaptations you've already made or plan.

Religious Routines/Rituals	Non-Religious Adaptations
Morning Devotions	Morning meditation
Periodic prayers	Periodic centering
Table blessings	Words of gratitude
Reading Holy Writings	Reading Inspirational Writings
Religious study	Book clubs, discussion groups
Listening to religious talks	Listening to Ted Talks
Bedtime prayers	Reflection
Tithing, almsgiving, charity	Intentional generosity
Dedicating an infant	Birthday party
Bar Mitzvah, First Communion	Coming of Age party
Marriage in a religious setting by a religious official	Marriage in a natural setting by a cherished friend
Last rites	Gathering of friends and family
Religious funeral	Memorial gathering

Again, this is not an exhaustive list. The routines and rituals of different religious traditions or communities vary widely. Regardless, there is little you did as a religious person you cannot continue doing with a new meaning or focus. The crucial question is what routines and rituals best serve you and your understanding of the world.

Identify four routines or rituals you found helpful or meaningful as a religious person:

1.

2.

3.

4.

Now identify the need these routines or rituals met. If you can't identify a corresponding need, consider the possibility you did what you did more out of religious obligation or habit than to meet a need. If you identified a deeper need, your task is not to replicate the religious routine or ritual – though often this works – but to find or create a new approach for meeting that need.

While adapting some religious routines as non-religious practices is common, be cautious about adapting every routine. One of the gifts of leaving religion is the opportunity and space to create different routines or rituals. There may be needs in your life that religion never met. Becoming non-religious may be the first time you've fully valued and acknowledged those needs.

"You know what I like to do on a Sunday morning? Clean my house. I really enjoy it; it's my ritual. I require tidiness, actually. I have to have everything spotless before I can relax."

-Jonathan Rhys Meyers

Making Moral Decisions

Religions often claim – without some divine authority or sanctioned code of behavior – non-religious people will be unequipped or incapable of making moral decisions, that all choices become relative and there is no means for determining what right from wrong. As with many religious opinions about a non-religious life, you have probably discovered this is wrong. Your ability to make thoughtful choices based on careful distinctions didn't disappear the day you left your religion. Indeed, you may have actually found decision making easier.

One of the often ignored complications with religious codes is the reliance on religious writings written in ancient cultures. Though there is wide uniformity on some of the larger ethical issues – murder, dishonesty, stealing and adultery – in all the religious writings, there is wide variation in the commands of various religions on many important ethical issues like human equality, human sexuality, justice, violence and tolerance.

Unfortunately, when you give allegiance to a religious code, most religions take responsibility for determining what to discard as archaic and what to enforce as divinely inspired. Your responsibility is to do as you are told whether it makes sense or not. This disconnect between what your religion told you and what you found compelling may have been one of the reasons you left religion.

A non-religious lifestyle is not an immoral one. Non-religious people have clear codes of conduct and strong opinions on what is right and wrong. One of the most common components of a non-religious code is the assumption that the noblest decisions are made without external coercion or compulsion, but because a person has carefully and intentionally chosen a course of action. What religion condemns as relativism is nothing more than a deep respect for the individuality and responsibility of each person.

All that being said, moving from a religious to a non-religious code of conduct can still be tricky. When you've been taught certain behaviors were acceptable or unacceptable since your childhood, separating indoctrination from personal opinion can be a challenge. Take a moment and review the following list of religious commands. Circle those you continue to value. Mark through any you find irrelevant or unnecessary. Star those you find immoral.

Do not murder	Forgive others
Be kind to your children	Defend the powerless
Do not work on the Sabbath	Never eat pork
Give to the poor	No sex outside of marriage
Wives should submit to husbands	Care for the sick and elderly
Do not steal	Cover your head
Honor your father and mother	Kill those who disbelieve in God
Worship God	Do not judge others
Do not lie.	Do not drink alcoholic beverages
Financially support religion	Obey your elders
Care for orphans and widows	Never cut your hair
Kill or ostracize homosexuals	Welcome the stranger
Pray five times a day	Take an eye for an eye
Love your neighbor as yourself	Love your enemies
Dress modestly	Be baptized
Cut your hair	Attend religious services
Do not gossip	Never divorce
Travel to Mecca once in your life	Visit people in prison
Circumcise male infants	Wash one another's feet
Do not commit adultery	Do not be jealous

What you have done in this exercise is what every person must do – be they religious or non-religious. Everyone must pick and choose between a vast array of opinions about what is good or bad. The difference between a religious code of conduct and a non-religious code of conduct is only that the non-religious person doesn't add, "Thus sayeth the Lord." The non-religious person take personal responsibility for their opinions, decisions and actions.

This doesn't mean morality is completely personal. A non-religious person will value many of the same ethical commands as the religious person. This agreement by vast numbers of people – religious and non-religious – about certain human values suggests morality does not require a religious underpinning. Humans are quite capable of identifying behaviors and actions that have nearly unanimous approval or disapproval. These codes can sometimes be very simple. The Hippocratic oath – "Do no harm" – is hard to beat.

Take a few minutes and write down your guiding principles. If this is difficult, you may want to explore some of the many non-religious ethical codes. If you can't create your own statement, find something that resonates with you. Remember, whatever you determine is not carved in stone or signed in blood. As a non-religious person, you are free to revise it based on your experiences in life.

"I reject any religious doctrine that does not appeal to reason and is in conflict with morality."

-Mahatma Gandhi

A Non-Religious Code

This is what you shall do;

Love the earth and sun and the animals,
despise riches,
give alms to every one that asks,
stand up for the stupid and crazy,
devote your income and labor to others,
hate tyrants,
argue not concerning God,
have patience and indulgence toward people,
take off your hat to nothing known or unknown or to any
man or number of men,
go freely with powerful uneducated persons and with the
young and with the mothers of families,
read these leaves in the open air every season of every year
of your life,
re-examine all you have been told at school or church or in
any book,
dismiss whatever insults your own soul,
and your very flesh shall be a great poem
and have the richest fluency not only in its words
but in the silent lines of its lips and face
and between the lashes of your eyes
and in every motion and joint of your body.

-Walt Whitman

Identifying New Heroes

Those leaving a religious tradition or community often claim to be followers of their religion's founder – be it Jesus, Moses, Mohammed, Buddha or the like – rather than a member of the religion. If you've made that distinction, you were probably hoping that by following the simple example of the founder of the religion you could disconnect from the ideas and practices you found troubling in the religion.

Unfortunately, if your guiding principle has been "What Would Jesus Do?" or the like, you face several problems. What know about your religion's founder has already been carefully manipulated and molded by your religious tradition. Unless the founder of your religion is alive and available for questioning, you have no certainty about what they would do or not do. Even if you could discover their opinion on every subject, you might ignore much of their advice. All religious figures are bound by their time and culture. They should not be expected to understand or anticipate every modern dilemma. That any single person should be an example for how you think and live is a religious belief. As a non-religious person, your goal is not to find someone to imitate, but to fully explore the unique and wonderful person that is you.

This doesn't mean a non-religious person has no heroes. You simply seek a different kind of person for inspiration. The following criteria may help you identify such people.

1. They claim no special revelation or divine authority for their thoughts and actions. What they think or do is attractive based on its merits.
2. They respect your autonomy and appreciate your point of view. They hope to learn important lessons from you, even as they share their expertise or knowledge.
3. They encourage you to explore where they haven't gone and think outside their box. They don't bind you to themselves and expect you to forever travel with them.

4. They admit the possibility that what they think or how they act could be wrong, for themselves or for others.

This is the kind of person you seek. They are heroic not in their ability to do what you can't, but in their willingness to courageously do what you resist and explore where you still fear. They offer an approach to life rather than a set of behaviors to imitate. They don't seek followers as much as fellow travelers.

Finding such people on your journey through life is not easy. Those who loudly and publicly claim to be such are already suspicious. The person you suspect of these characteristics will be quietly sitting by a stream or strolling through the woods, reflecting on their own life, intent on exploring rather than gathering a band. When you encounter such a person either in writing or in person, enjoy their company for a time. Learn what you can from watching them. Be prepared for the day when they take a fork in the path you would not choose and – on that day – bid them a kind farewell.

Take a moment to write down one or two people who might fit this description for you.

If you don't recognize such a person in your life presently, don't be too concerned. Though you will probably encounter people like this as you explore the world, don't make finding them your goal. Instead of looking for new heroes, become the hero you've imagined and sought.

"A hero is someone who understands the responsibility that comes with his freedom."

-Bob Dylan

Non-Religious Introspection

Religions — at their best — ask important questions about the purpose and qualities of a good life. They ask you to look within, acknowledge your faults and shortcomings, and seek to be a better person. Ironically, in many cases, your religious community taught you the very practices that eventually led you to leave that religious community. One day, when you looked within, you realized one of your shortcomings was your failure to abandon inadequate beliefs and practices. You decided your best bet for becoming a better person was outside a religious context.

What you reject in becoming non-religious is not the need for periodic and intentional introspection, but the insistence religion is the only or best place to do this important practice. Truth be told, introspection created religion and not the other way around. Religious beliefs are simply the honored opinions of reflective people about the purpose and qualities of a good life. While the answers of these past philosophers have value, the necessity of introspection is the underlying lesson.

Unfortunately, in leaving your religious community, you may have also left your primary setting for introspection. There may be no other place where you can presently go and talk about deep issues and questions with others who share that same interest. If so, this isn't easy to find or create. If you live in a large city, there are probably non-religious groups with regular meetings, lectures and forums. If not, you may need to identify other non-religious people and ask them if they'd like to meet periodically for introspective discussion.

Be careful about what you join. The more institutional the non-religious organization, the more it will act like a religion. While this may feel familiar, joining another group of people with a prescribed set of answers for all the important questions is simply climbing a different mountain. Just as some non-religious paths are more dangerous than others, not all non-religious groups are healthy and helpful. The questions you used to identify new heroes can also be used to eliminate certain groups.

1. Do they claim no special knowledge or authority?
2. Do they respect your autonomy and opinion?
3. Do they require no promises or long term commitments?
4. Do they present their opinions humbly and tentatively?

If so, they may be good people with whom to continue your introspection. If not, beware. You may need to create what you cannot find.

Be careful about what you create. Most religions probably began as informal gatherings of thoughtful people looking for alternative answers. If you gather others to think and discuss, recognize your tendency to recreate what you previously knew – something that looks much like the religion you left. Though you should be cautious, this temptation to replicate your religion is not a reason to avoid creating non-religious groups. There is value in testing your opinions on important questions against the opinions of others.

It may be healthy for whatever group you create to periodically ask itself, "Why do we gather?" Answering that question will help you and others determine what needs the group is meeting or what they are not. Communities form around a variety of legitimate needs. If your pressing need is introspection, make certain what you create meets that need.

One distinct possibility – as you sort through how best to meet your need for introspection – is that you left religion precisely because you no longer need to do your introspection with a tour group and a chaperone. You may be ready to explore on your own. You may not expect any single approach, place or people to meet your need for introspection. The journey within is a journey you're willing to take alone.

"The more powerful and original a mind, the more it will incline towards the religion of solitude."

-Aldous Huxley

Contributing to the World

The giving of yourself to other people or to a greater purpose is a widely acclaimed human value and not uniquely religious. Many people do wonderful things in the world without a religious motive and without needing or expecting divine approval. When religious people dismiss acts of kindness and compassion because they lack religious trappings, they expose two ugly realities about religious acts of charity.

The first is the pervasive religious assumption that giving your time, money and talents is a divine expectation and religious obligation. Generosity is not acknowledged as an innate human value. It must be commanded and rewarded. Religion often suggests that, if left to your own devices, you wouldn't give of yourself.

Unfortunately, when religion assumes this about human nature, it strips much of the wonder and power from generosity. The religious imperative takes what was meant as a gift and makes it into a transaction. You bless others in order to be blessed or to avoid punishment. When you first left your religious community, if you quit giving of your time, money and talent, you may have been caught in this kind of thinking. Without the command and promised reward, you may have discovered you were not nearly as generous as you thought.

Hopefully, this was not the case. You are probably a person who finds great happiness and satisfaction in bettering the world. Most people do. If you struggled with how to give of your time, money and talent after you left your religious community, it was probably because you relied so completely upon them to define and direct your generosity.

The second ugly reality of religious charity is that your trust was betrayed – most of what religions call charity isn't. While nearly every religion includes an obligation to care for the poor, oppressed and downtrodden, most religions devote a vast majority of their time, money and talent to the mission of recruiting new members. Indeed, in most religious traditions, one of the clearly stated objectives of the religion is to convert – sometimes by any means possible – every person in the world. Though this command to conquer is downplayed in many religious communities, the core mission of most religion remains to perpetuate itself.

If you were heavily involved in the religious activities of your religious community and if you gave significant dollars, you may recognize what religions seldom admit – ninety percent of the time, money and talent you gave to your religious tradition was invested in services and amenities designed to meet your needs or recruit others to the community. While there are certainly exceptions, very little of what most religious communities do or the money they donate has any impact on addressing issues of inequality or injustice.

In leaving your religious community, you essentially cut out the middleman, eliminated your membership fees and freed yourself to more directly and effectively give your time, money and talents to people and causes that deeply matter to you. The challenge is in determining how and to whom you give. No longer do you abdicate your personal responsibility by giving a donation to your religious community. The money and the responsibility belong to you.

This can feel like a heavy responsibility. How can you responsibly donate the hundreds or thousands of dollars you once gave to and through your religious community? You may have to do some research and seek out new avenues for giving. Take the time to carefully think about how you'd like to use your money. Answer the following questions:

1. When you were religious, what causes or people did you most enjoy financially supporting?

2. When you were religious, what causes or people did you wish your religious community had supported more fully?

3. What are the causes or who are the people that intrigue or inspire you?

Ultimately, giving should not feel like a heavy responsibility. It should be an opportunity to invest in what matters to you. If you're still feeling obligated to give, you may still be operating out of some residual religious guilt. Giving should be fun and gratifying. If it isn't, something is wrong.

As a non-religious person, you're giving may look very different. It may not be monthly gifts to the same organizations. You may give much more broadly, responding to the needs or concerns you encounter. Your giving may not always be tax-deductible. You may have close friends and family that could use your support. You may help someone go to college or start a new business.

Don't limit your giving to causes. Look for opportunities to personally engage. Though religions also encourage this kind of engagement, it is often tainted by an underlying motivation to recruit someone. You are now free to relate to people without strings attached. Find people being impacted by the problems you care about and give to them directly. Build relationships. Give of your time as well as your money.

Remember, your task as a non-religious person is to explore the world; not to save it. One way of doing this is by visiting places vastly different than where you've lived and meeting people with struggles and challenges you've never faced. Sometimes you need to pitch your tent in places that – though initially unattractive – only reveal their beauty to those willing to look more deeply. Sometimes you need to travel with people – who though they may slow your pace – eventually teach you more about the journey and yourself.

As you explore the world, make commitments. Do no damage. Repair what you can. Pick up your trash and the trash of others. Help those you meet along your path. Leave every place you visit slightly better than when you came. If you do these things, you will be a generous person.

"I hate the giving of a hand unless the whole man accompanies it."

-Ralph Waldo Emerson

You've traveled far from the mountain.

You're no longer looking back with loss or nostalgia.

You're speaking a new language
with less and less accent.

You are identifying yourself
as a non-religious person.

You're taking personal responsibility for
meeting your needs in non-religious ways.

Your final challenge
is revising the story you tell
about yourself
and the world.

This is no easy task.
It must be a story simple enough
to share with your children,
yet complex enough to communicate
your unique perspective and place in the world.

"Man is the only animal for whom his own existence
is a problem he has to solve."

-Erich Fromm

Revising Your Story

Since the first day you began putting words into sentences, you have been creating – whether you realized it or not – a personal story. Through thousands of questions and millions of observations you've developed a narrative for understanding yourself and your place in the world, for explaining how and why you exist. Throughout your life, you have continually revised that story to better reflect your experiences, replacing inadequate story lines with more plausible ones, reinterpreting past experiences based on new knowledge and self-awareness.

When your parents first told you of Santa Claus and reindeer and gifts brought down a chimney, you didn't question their narrative. You incorporated that story into your own even if your house didn't have a chimney. It adequately accounted for the presents under the tree. Only when the implausibility of that story line became too great, did you revise it, developing better explanations for what happened on Christmas Eve. What you did with Santa Claus, you've done with much of your religious story.

At an early age, your religious community offered you an all-encompassing story, designed to respond to every childhood question with some definitive answer. You probably incorporated many of its story lines into your own without much thought. Young and inexperienced, one explanation for the way the world began, operated or ended seemed as plausible as another. If you were raised in a religious setting, your personal story was infused with religious assumptions, images, personalities and hopes, some of which gradually became less and less plausible.

Though leaving your religion usually requires significant revisions of your personal story, you don't start from scratch. You've been reinterpreting religious story lines for years. You've eliminated the objectionable and implausible, edited the plot and reimagined some of the central characters. You've incorporated aspects of other stories, religious or otherwise, weaving these alternate narratives into the fabric of your story, replacing what became ridiculous or ugly with something you found more helpful or beautiful, until your

165

personal story may bear little resemblance to your religion's story. These gradual revisions have prepared you for the rewriting necessary when you finally leave a religious tradition.

In the following pages, you'll have the opportunity of revising your personal story once again, of creating a post-religious version that better reflects your present understanding of the world and of reinterpreting past experiences in the light of how you presently understand yourself. In so doing, you may also develop a story you feel more comfortable sharing with others, and more importantly, passing onto your children and grandchildren.

Using Your Razor

Thomas Jefferson is famous as a founding father, the chief author of the Declaration of Independence and the third President of the United States. A lesser known fact about Jefferson was his creation of an alternative version of the Christian story. In the early 1800s, Jefferson took a razor to the Christian scriptures and glued bits and pieces into a document he entitled *The Life and Morals of Jesus of Nazareth*. In creating his Jeffersonian Bible, he excluded miracles and supernatural acts, eliminated the resurrection and removed any claims of Jesus' divinity. Though published long after his death, it clearly represents one man's attempt to revise the religious content of his personal story.

Though you may not take a razor to your religion's writings, in leaving your religion, your personal story probably needs some editing and rewriting. Though being non-religious doesn't require the rejection of every religious opinion, you may still discover lingering assumptions, speculations and narratives that need to go. Eliminating or reinterpreting the offensive, inhibiting or implausible will give your personal story more clarity and integrity.

Review the following list of common religious assumptions, speculations and narratives. Cross out those you have abandoned or wish to eliminate from your personal story.

God exists

God created the universe and world

God created the universe quickly and recently

God created the universe over billions of years

The world and everything in it was created perfect.

The world and everything in it became tainted

God interacts with people

God speaks primarily through a few special humans

God speaks to every person

God sometimes takes human form

There are unseen spirits, angels, or demons in the world

Some writings are holy and without error

Some writings are inspired by God

There are certain rituals and rule keeping necessary for pleasing God

There is an evil force at work against the divine purpose

People must be forgiven, saved, redeemed, or purified

God determines everything that happens

Everything happens for a reason

Each person has a special role in a divine plan

Prayer alters events and situations

God can intervene in any situation or event

God sometimes violates the laws of nature

Those who serve God will be blessed and protected in this life

Those who serve God in this life – though they may not be blessed or protected – will be rewarded in the next.

There is life after this life

People are reincarnated in a new form or body

God will judge all humanity

Heaven or paradise is the reward for the righteous

Hell is the punishment for the wicked

Review each statement you crossed out and write your opinion or explanation below it. When you are unable to provide either, circle the statement. This may represent a gap in your present understanding of the world as well as a focus for future exploration. Figuring out how to explain the mysterious is part of the non-religious adventure.

Now examine those statements you didn't cross out. These are religious opinions or explanations you still find credible or plausible. Look at each one and ask yourself whether this religious opinion is still deeply compelling or whether it is merely a placeholder until something better comes along.

In this exercise, you've identified four different types of story lines:

1. Stories that still have power and meaning for you.
2. Stories that, though problematic, are better than your other options.
3. Stories that are no longer plausible but have not been replaced.
4. New stories with power and meaning.

These four types of story lines represent a snapshot of how you're presently revising your personal story. While a few stories may remain powerful for your entire life, many of the stories you find helpful at one point of your life become problematic as you mature. Stories go from meaningful to inadequate to unsatisfactory to being replaced. Your understanding of yourself and your place in the world evolves. This is also true of your understanding of God.

Rewriting the Central Character

Take a moment and notice how many of the statements about God are no longer meaningful to you. As a non-religious person, you may have crossed out many or all of the statements about God. This represents another significant shift. At some point in the revision of your personal story, though the past events of your life remained the same, the central character of that story changed. Instead of God, it became you.

Though identifying yourself as the central character of your own story may seem obvious, accepting this role is often difficult for people raised in a religious culture. As a religious person, your personal story was a small tale in a cosmic drama. In that epic, you were never the central character. Your role was to worship and obey, to play some small part in advancing a plan designed to glorify God. You were a child or servant of God. You were a disciple, worshipper, or follower. God was the star and you were an extra.

As a non-religious person, you've altered, diminished or even eliminated the role of God in your life. Your personal story is about you. Even if you continue to include God or something like God, you are the one writing, directing and starring. You've stepped out of the chorus and taken the lead. You determine the actions, the words, the themes, the events, the co-stars and the scenery. You choose the role you play. If you choose, your personal story can be about a strong, heroic, independent and responsible adult, capable of making decisions, of being happy and authentic.

Hopefully, this isn't a difficult role for you to play. If you reflect, you've been taking on more and more of that role since the moment you walked away from your religion. What is sometimes more difficult is intentionally revising your story to reflect who you've become and publicly acknowledging yourself as the central character.

As a religious person, you were probably taught such a claim was arrogant at best and downright sinful at worst. In Christianity, the arch villain is an angel who claimed independence from God. In many religions, humility, self-denial and submission are lifted up as high virtues. If you were raised in this culture, though you may have already taken personal responsibility for your life, you may still be reluctant to publicly assert your full independence. Though you've written the story, you may still feel obligated to list the authorship as God. At the very least, give yourself equal billing. Becoming the central character of a story about you is not selfish or sinful, but an act of maturity and self-respect.

Once you make this shift in perspective, you will be better equipped to revise the past, interpret the present and create the future. You'll be ready to offer a more personally authentic explanation of beginnings, endings and much of what happens in between, always remembering these significant differences between religious and non-religious stories.

1. Religions offer all-encompassing narratives with definitive answers to every existential question. Your personal story may always have gaps. While you may ultimately decide to fill

these gaps with personal opinion or speculation, it is perfectly acceptable to conclude "It's a mystery" or "I don't know."

2. Religions emphasize a single source of knowledge, usually called God. Your personal story may incorporate thoughts and ideas from a variety of sources and make no claim to ultimate authority.

3. Religions argue their story is the only legitimate story. Your personal story is exactly that – personal. There is no need for you to convince others to adopt your story.

On the other hand, having a story that makes sense both to you and others is also gratifying. For thousands of years, humans have sat around fires, looked up at the stars and asked questions of origins, meaning and destiny. A vast number of explanations have been told around those fires. Some of those stories were so compelling they've been retold time and again. Though religions have repeatedly tried to shut down this questioning and storytelling as no longer necessary, they have failed. You have just as much right to offer your opinion as anyone in history.

Rewriting the Plot

Most stories have a beginning, middle and end. They are designed in such a way because humans are generally dissatisfied with stories without these three elements. Religious stories – in their obsession with certainty – usually offer a definitive starting point, a clear plot and a climactic ending. Your personal story – as a non-religious one – is not bound by such tight constraints, but it is helpful to think carefully about each of these elements as you create a post-religious story.

The Beginning

Nearly every child eventually asks when and how the universe began. For millennia, one person's guess was as good as another. Every explanation was speculation. Though religions claimed special knowledge, religious explanations differed. Even within a single religious tradition, there has been debate. The Book of Genesis offers two distinct and different stories of creation.

No religion can claim definitive proof of how it all began. Neither can science. The Big Bang is a theory. While there is growing evidence to support this explanation, theories are continually revised and refined. There are no eyewitnesses to the creation of the universe, nor is there an answer to the question of what created whatever existed before the Big Bang. The most honest introduction to a creation story is probably "once upon a time" rather than "in the beginning."

That being said, there is universal curiosity about beginnings. Every religion and culture has offered an explanation. Nearly every one of these stories attempts to answer one or both of the following questions. Take a moment to answer them yourself. In this case, don't answer "I don't know." No one knows. Offer your opinion.

1. Was the creation of the universe a random or purposeful act?

2. Is the universe inherently good, bad or morally neutral?

As a non-religious person, the point of this exercise is not to choose the right answer, but to explore how you presently view the world. Your opinion says far more about you than it does about the creation of the universe. It reveals your assumptions about everything that has happened, is happening, or will happen. How you understand the beginning of life often influences how you understand the end.

The End

The ultimate existential question has always been what happens when you die. Do you cease to exist or continue in some new form or place? As with questions of beginning, there are lots of theories and stories. While religions are fairly uniform in their assurance of an afterlife, what they describe varies widely. Some offer physical resurrection or spiritual transformation. Others argue for earthly reincarnation. Some even promise eventual divinity.

This wide variety in the descriptions of the afterlife suggests no one really knows. While many religions claim the resurrection or reincarnation of significant historic figures, few people claim to have received any words of assurance from beyond the grave. This alone is not an argument against the possibility of an afterlife, but it suggests most people – if they believe in the afterlife – hold that belief without any experiential evidence. They take it on faith.

As a non-religious person, you need to ask yourself this question:

If there isn't an afterlife, does this alter my behavior or change my purpose in life?

If not, what you think about the afterlife probably isn't terribly important. If you find the hope of an afterlife attractive, keep hoping. Share this hope with others. If you find the hope of an afterlife unnecessary, be humble. Your ability to live life without this hope may be a lack of imagination rather than a sign of genius.

However, if the lack of an afterlife would alter your behavior or change your purpose in life, this is a more difficult issue. This suggests, without a carrot and a stick, you would live differently. You may be denying yourself some present happiness in hopes of some future reward. Your belief in an afterlife may actually be diminishing the quality of your life. Hoping for an afterlife is harmless. Depending on an afterlife to give your life meaning or meet your needs is not.

There is one last reason many retain a belief in the afterlife. When people you deeply love die, it is difficult to accept you may never see them again. If this is your situation, think carefully about your motives. Is your belief in the afterlife a hope or an attempt to deny death or to negotiate with it? Again, hoping for an afterlife can be comforting. Depending on an afterlife to resolve your feelings of loss and sadness isn't healthy.

In the end, what is most impressive in a human life is not what you think about death, but how you approach it. You don't usually get to write the end of your personal story. Death is beyond your control, but what you do with your life is largely in your hands. Those who focus on the afterlife often miss some of the joys of this life. If you can give each day of your life your fullest attention, you will know happiness and the world will mourn your death. Be careful that your fascination with the beginning and end of life doesn't keep you from fully appreciating the middle.

The Middle

The middle of a story is where everything happens. Though much of who we are is determined by genetics and upbringing, the middle of a story is where you have the most control. As a responsible adult, you write this part of your personal story. You're born. You grow up. You make decisions. You choose friends and partners. You set goals and define your purpose. You live life – sometimes successfully and sometimes disastrously. You reflect and change. You mature. This is the plot of most human stories, be they religious or otherwise.

What differs from story to story is mostly the commentary. How do you understand your presence in the world? How does this understanding influence your decisions, choices and goals? What does it mean to live a successful life, to grow old gracefully?

As you should expect, religions are as definitive about the answers to these questions as they are about those of beginnings and ends. The religious answers about the purpose of life are often built on assumptions about the creation and destiny. In many religions, the universe is not morally neutral. There are forces of good and evil competing for your allegiance. Without divine assistance or rescue, you have little hope of choosing correctly or living life well.

As a non-religious person, you have probably come to doubt some or all of these religious assumptions about the character of the world and the purpose of life. This does not mean you must live a life without meaning. In becoming non-religious, you simply have the choice to reject story lines that limited your roles to sinner or saint, rebel or servant. Your purpose in life need not be part of some cosmic battle between good and evil.

Take a moment and give your best answers to the following questions.

1. Into what kind of world were you born?

2. What difference does your presence in the world make?

3. How do you determine the best choices and goals?

4. How do you judge if your life is successful?

If you found answering these questions difficult, don't be discouraged. They are hard questions, especially when you no longer answer them with religious platitudes. It could take months or even years to develop satisfying answers. Be patient. The response "I'm working on that" is acceptable.

A non-religious life can answer each of these questions in a way both personally gratifying and socially admirable. You don't require God or religion to give meaning to your life. You can create purpose for yourself. You can give commentary to all that has happened, is happening and will happen without needing to rely on a religious story.

This may be one of the richest challenges of the non-religious life. You, and you alone, get to determine the meaning of your life. You, and your alone, get to judge whether your life was meaningful. Once you've revised your personal story and eliminated unhelpful religious story lines, you are ready to live an uninhibited non-religious life.

From this day forward you can begin the writing of a post-religious story, the story of someone who no longer walks in the shadow of the mountain. Though your religious history will always be a part of your personal story, it no longer defines who you are, what you do or where you go. You are free to explore, create, reflect, engage, celebrate and evolve, to seek your deepest happiness and satisfaction, to be your most authentic self.

"It's like everyone tells a story about themselves inside their own head. Always. All the time. That story makes you what you are. We build ourselves out of that story."

-Patrick Rothfuss

Take a moment and turn back
to the questions on page 92-93.

Ask yourself those questions again.

Hopefully, you're now able to say "yes"
to most or even all of those statements.

If not...
you may want to reread this section of the book,
take more time with some of the exercises,
and give the questions more thought.

Though you're probably not returning to religion,
you may want to put this book down for a while.

There is no hurry.
The transition from being religious
to being non-religious can take years for some.

However...
if you're no longer walking in the shadow of the mountain,
if you're bored with talking about your religious past,
if verbs like exploring, creating, rethinking, engaging,
and evolving fill you with excitement,
read on.

The adventure is just beginning.

Part Three

Moving

Forward

What Have You Become?

It is never easy to identify or explain yourself when you're in the midst of a major transition. Since how you understand yourself may shift from day to day, you may find yourself using one description in the morning and a different one in the afternoon. How you perceive yourself may change dependent on your mood, need, audience and most recent experience. In this book, the term "non-religious" has been offered as a helpful and temporary placeholder, though it may become less satisfying the further you're removed from religion.

Calling yourself non-religious is problematic because it still defines you by what you are not rather than by what you are becoming, what you are, or what you wish to be. Atheist, agnostic and other non-religious terms share this same flaw. They imply religion is normative and everything else an odd aberration. If your identity relies on religion as a foil, no matter how far you move away, you never completely escape the shadow of the mountain.

And yet – if religion has been a major part of your life – adopting an identity without reference to religion is also inaccurate. A truly non-religious person is someone who grew up without a religious tradition or community. When asked about their religious affiliation, identifying as non-religious tells their whole story. They have never understood themselves in relationship to a religious framework. This is not true for you.

You are more post-religious than non-religious. Non-religious describes your present perspective on life, but post-religious better defines your history and how you've changed. In this final section of the book, non-religious will be reserved for those aspects of life you share with those who've never claimed a religious affiliation. Post-religious will be used when describing moments and experiences connected to your religious past. Understanding this distinction is an indication of how far you've come, that you're comfortable with who you were and who you are. You can look back without regret and forward with confidence and anticipation.

No matter how you identify yourself
one thing is certain:
you couldn't go back to your religion
even if you tried.

And you don't want to go back.
You want to move forward,
to explore uncharted territory,
to go where you've never been before.

There are wonders
to see, hear and touch.

There are people, places and experiences
that will take your breath away.

There are thoughts you'll think for the very first time,
sentences you'll form that you've never formed before,
conversations you'll have that were once taboo.
Anything and everything is possible.

There is no more loss and much less struggle.
You're ready to explore.

You're happy.

"While I am opposed to all orthodox creeds, I have a creed myself;
and my creed is this. Happiness is the only good. The time to be
happy is now. The place to be happy is here."

-Robert Ingersoll

Happiness

In the beginning of this book, you were asked to answer a series of questions about your happiness and satisfaction with your religious community, its practices and its beliefs. Since you've read this far, it's probably safe to assume your answers exposed some deep unhappiness with your religious tradition. If you've left your religious tradition and worked through this book carefully and intentionally, you're hopefully much less dissatisfied. You're probably feeling more authentic. You're becoming happier.

While it is difficult to be happy when your head, heart and actions are out of sync, authenticity and happiness – while connected - are not exactly the same. Becoming post-religious does not automatically result in a deep satisfaction with your life. In leaving your religious tradition, stripping your life of religious vestiges and ridding your mind of religious assumptions, you've simply cleared space for something new. Though there is power in such moments in life, your level of happiness and satisfaction from here on is largely dependent upon the choices you make.

As you make these important decisions, remember you are the best equipped to know what will bring you happiness. You, and you alone, are ultimately responsible for your satisfaction with life. Whenever you forget these truths, expect to become unhappy. Though others can certainly accompany and assist you in reflecting, exploring and learning, it should be you who determines your future.

In this final section of the book, you'll be presented with many exciting possibilities and opportunities. Some of these ideas may seem intriguing. Others may seem odd. Use and adapt what works. Reject what doesn't. Don't approach these suggestions as a to-do list, but as helpful prods to your own creativity. What will make you the happiest is when you discover something uniquely you.

As in the previous sections, you'll be asked to think carefully and intentionally about where you are, what you desire and how you should move forward. The options are nearly unlimited. Your challenge will be in determining which of the possible paths is most likely to lead to your greater happiness. Since life is a journey, you'll need to make this decision whenever there is a fork in the road.

In preparation for this repeated task of decision making, take a moment and complete the following statements. Don't limit yourself to a single word, sentence or sentiment. Hopefully, there are a variety of ways you could complete each statement.

1.   I am most happy in places that...

2.   I am most happy when I am...

3.   I am most happy with people who...

These statements offer important clues to which paths you should take and which you should ignore. Look for whatever intrigues or thrills. Avoid places, actions, or groups that don't match these statements or might cause harm to you or others. Exploring and experimenting is wonderful, but deciding to accompany a beekeeper on a trip to harvest honey from a beehive might not be wise if you're highly allergic to bee stings.

Be curious. Be brave. Be careful.

Most of all, be happy.

"It's a helluva start, being able to recognize what makes you happy."

-Lucille Ball

For the post-religious person,
there is one belief that matters most.

It is absolutely crucial you believe
you are an independent and responsible adult,
capable of setting your own course,
making your own decisions
and trusting your own intuition.

You can go any place and do anything
that interests you.

You decide
what is important,
what is valuable,
what is worth examining
and what is worth learning.

Unexplored physical, emotional, intellectual,
cultural, psychological and social worlds
are open to you.

Your opportunities and possibilities are nearly infinite.

You are limited only
by your personal constraints
and a lack of imagination.

Do you believe in yourself?

Explore, Discover, Examine, Learn

One of the truest indicators of whether you've become a post-religious person may be your ability to hear a proclamation of personal autonomy as good news. Hopefully, you are thrilled by your freedom to act, feel, think, say and engage in ways you've never done before. Though you won't choose to do everything, you can consider anything.

Unfortunately, when you're coming out of years of religious life, this sudden overabundance of options can be a little overwhelming. Like an immigrant visiting Wal-Mart for the first time, you may not know how to handle going from having one choice in cereal to having a hundred brands to choose from. It takes time to completely believe, accept and embrace your freedom. Remember, though you are free to do anything, you don't have to do it all tomorrow. Don't allow the plethora of possibilities to paralyze you. Don't make being post-religious a chore or an obligation.

When it comes to exploring, about any direction is as good as another. As long as you're going where you haven't gone or doing what you've never done, you are creating the possibility of something heart and mind expanding. If there are questions that beg answers, you can explore how others have answered them. If there are experiences you've envied, try them. If there are places you've wanted to go, go.

The following lists of possibilities – divided into three categories – offer you some simple first steps. They are intended to spur your own imagination and creativity.

Explore Different Thoughts

- Make a list of unanswered questions you've always had about yourself or the world. Pick one or two of the most pressing or interesting and start looking for answers. Put your question into an internet search engine and see where it takes you.

- Study the creation myths of different cultures. Choose the one you find most beautiful. Study evolution, the Big Bang theory, quantum physics, chaos theory or some other scientific thread. Determine what scientific explanations you find most compelling. Consider writing your own story of beginnings.

- Read books about the many ways people have imagined the afterlife. Learn about reincarnation. Examine end of life experiences. Decide which speculations about the afterlife are the most plausible to you and which ones seem the most fantastic.

- Audit a philosophy class at a local university. Read what they are reading and join in the discussion. Discover how others have ordered their world and understood meaning and purpose. Determine which ideas are nearly universal and which seem a matter of personal preference.

- List and examine the ideas, experiences and places you still find taboo. Explore how others think about them. Decide what is prejudice, what is personal preference and what is an ethical qualm. Overcome your prejudices.

- Find websites, blogs or podcasts that explore issues and questions from a non-religious perspective. Watch the top twenty TED Talks and discover what millions of people are thinking about.

- Seek out people you respect who weren't raised in a religious community. Ask them about how they understand themselves and the world. Explore how people without a religious point of reference order their lives.

- Read a book on human psychology or self-improvement. Learn how humans develop. Study Maslov's Hierarchy of Needs and see where you fit.

Explore Different Experiences

- Make a list of experiences you've always envied or desired – a personal bucket list. Pick one or two of the lowest hanging fruit and take a bite. Once you whet your appetite for the new and unusual, you may find exploration and discovery easier and easier.

- Read *Faith No More* by Phil Zuckerman. (Oxford Univ. Press, 2011). This book explores the diverse motives and approaches to leaving religion through interviews with people who have left a variety of religious traditions and communities. As a post-religious person, you may find the experiences of others who've left religion fascinating.

- Read about other religious traditions, beliefs and practices. Visit one of their services. Remember, you are not anti-religious. As a non-religious person, you're actually much better equipped to observe objectively. Discover the similarities and differences between other religions and what you experienced. Consider the plausibility of alternate beliefs. Adopt or adapt practices you find interesting.

- Find out if you're an atheist. Read *Atheism: A Very Short Introduction* by Julian Baggini. This short well written book should help you figure out what you think or don't think about God. If you still believe in God, define what you mean by God.

- Begin reading atheist writers like Sam Harris, Richard Dawkins or Christopher Hitchens. Delve into more classical writings like Robert Ingersoll, Bertrand Russell, George Santayana, Friedrich Nietzsche or Lucretius. Even if you continue to believe in God, understanding why many don't is still helpful.

- Do something you always thought harmless or intriguing, but that your religious community prohibited. Have a glass of good wine. Go dancing. Eat pork.. Drink caffeine. Get a tattoo. Wear different clothing. Cut your hair. Grow your hair. Have fun sex.

Explore Different Places

- Make a list of books, movies or plays your religion prohibited or denigrated. Read, watch or go see the ones that intrigue you. Sometimes the first and easiest way to visit different places is through books, movies and plays.

- Attend a TED Talks or TEDx conference in a city near you. Look for conferences, workshops and lectures about different ideas or experiences. Use some of the money you once invested in religious institutions to fund your own mind expansion.

- Plan a trip or vacation to another country and culture. Skip the resorts and look for ways to live with, meet and interact with the people of that place. Study the culture and the ways they approach life differently than you. Consider what they might understand better than you do.

- If you live in a city, get out of the city. If you live in the country or a small town, spend time in the city. Visit places where you're in the minority. Attend an event to see how others think rather than to reconfirm your opinions

- If you harbor deep anger or resentment toward your religious tradition or community, seek out counseling. There was probably emotional damage you need to repair. Leaving does not automatically heal these wounds. Be willing to visit unchartered territory within yourself.

- Even if you're not angry, consider counseling or a life coach. If you've avoided therapy or personal reflection, explore the possibility that talking to an objective person about your life might be helpful. See it as an investment in your own happiness.

Maybe all of these suggestions seem interesting. If so, choose one or two and begin there. They will lead to other opportunities. If none of these ideas seem intriguing, think about what and how you would like to explore. If the whole process seems overwhelming or exhausting, don't panic. You may need some time to breathe before exploring a new trail. Relax. Remember, these are options and not obligations.

If you do choose to pursue one of these suggestions, don't worry about choosing incorrectly. Some paths turn out to be dead ends. Some thoughts and ideas, once explored, will prove inadequate and unsatisfying. You won't always make the right choice. This is not evidence of your lack of decision making ability or of a need for another external authority. This is part of being an adult. Whatever choices you make – right or wrong - are your choices. Glory in them. As you move forward, you'll get more comfortable with making your own decisions and claiming your autonomy. Eventually, you will guard it fiercely and without apology.

There is nothing more valuable than your right to freely explore this world. Oppose every effort by governments, institutions or other people to diminish or limit this freedom. Support and applaud groups and people who risk much in order to expose others to alternative ideas, experiences and places. Understand exploration as much more than an extracurricular activity. Exploration is an essential component of a happy life.

"This I believe: that the free, exploring mind of the individual human is the most valuable thing in the world."

–John Steinbeck

As you explore
new thoughts, experiences and places,
sometimes you discover
nothing quite meets your needs or desires.

This is not cause for despair.

This is an invitation
to personal creativity,
imagination
and experimentation.

You are a creator,
capable of imaging new ideas,
of experimenting
and of creating your own place in this world

What you can't find
you can create.

As you learn to appreciate
your unique perspective and personality,
you will become more confident
when required to create.

Indeed, with time,
you may see creation
as more exciting than exploration.

Create, Imagine, Experiment

Early in your post-religious life, you will probably explore more than you create. This is normal and understandable. It takes a lot of energy to walk away from your religion. There may not be much left for creativity. When you come to a fork in the road, you'll choose a well-traveled path. This is still exciting. While you may not be blazing a new trail, the trail will be new for you.

Avoid the trap of seeing every fork in the road as having only two options – the religious or non-religious path. As a post-religious person, you may be especially susceptible to seeing the world as black and white, right and wrong or good and evil. Initially, on important existential questions, you may be tempted to think there are only two choices – religion is good or evil, God exists or doesn't exist, morality is absolute or completely relative. These are all well-traveled paths. You've already walked one of the options. You may choose to explore the opposite, but be careful. Limiting every decision to either north or south ignores east and west and every other directional variation.

When faced with dueling opinions, consider the possibility there might be a third, fourth or fifth path. As you explore, you will hopefully encounter situations where none of the well-traveled paths seem all that compelling. See this as a positive development. You're beginning to better understand yourself and your unique interests and needs. The well-traveled paths of others may no longer satisfy you. Eventually – out of desire or necessity - you may choose to step off the path and create your own way in the world.

You can and probably should create your own path. While some people are certainly more creative than others, creativity is a universal human skill. A lack of creativity is often the result of inexperience or low self-esteem rather than inability. You are capable of taking various ideas or objects, rearranging them and creating something unique and personal. You've done this all your life in myriad circumstances. Don't underestimate your ability to be creative.

What often keeps you from being creative about the deeper issues and questions of life may be an ingrained assumption that you have no right to stray from ancient, time tested paths, that unless thousands of others think what you think, act as you act or go where you go, then what you think, what you do or where you travel must be wrong. The challenge is often in seeing moments of personal inspiration or unique perspective as a cause for excitement and joy rather than fear and concern.

Once you make this shift, creativity, imagination and experimentation become less of a necessity and more of an act of autonomy. You create not because you have to, but because you want to. You choose a path not because it is the easiest, but because it is the most interesting. Though acts of creativity are more work, they also have the potential for greater personal satisfaction.

The following list offers you creative activities and exercises for reordering your life. As always, try what is helpful. Ignore what is not. If nothing resonates, be creative.

- Consider two common answers to a question that matters to you and write down what you find attractive in each answer. Instead of choosing one or the other, try to develop a third answer that combines the most attractive elements of both, or – better yet – create an answer that differs from both of them.

- List several events, routines or gatherings of people that presently have power and meaning for you. Create a calendar highlighting those moments and days. Give these events, routines or gatherings as much priority and value as you once gave to religious activities. Create rituals to honor and celebrate those moments.

- Listen to yourself over several days and write down religious words and phrases you catch yourself using. Develop alternatives that better represent your view of yourself and the world. Create a personal language for describing your approach to the world. Intentionally develop a better vocabulary.

- Spend some time reading about ethics and seeing how other people make moral decisions without reference to religion or God. Then, instead of adopting someone else's approach, write a personal code of conduct. Post it where you can read and review it every day. Test your ability to live by these values.

- Think about what is most important to you in life. What would you call someone with these values? Create and adopt an identity that describes and communicates what is important to you. Try using that identifier. How does that identity makes you feel? How do other people respond to it? Remember, you have the right to identify yourself any way you please.

- Identify the activities that presently bring you the most peace and relaxation. Define these activities as your core practices. If your life lacks moments of peace and relaxation, create moments. Defend that time as priority in your life.

- Create a post-religious narrative about your life. Why were you religious in the first place? What was positive about that background? What was problematic? Why did you leave? What did that accomplish? Write it down. Revisit it in six months or a year. Answer the questions again and see if your interpretation has changed.

In each of these examples, the goal is not to create something permanent or absolute, but to tailor something to your present perspective, needs and interests. In any decision making situation, when none of the options seem compelling, you are free to choose "none of the above." In so doing, you announce you desire to create, imagine and experiment.

Trust your gut. When you find the best path for you — be it through exploration or creation — it will feel more like walking downhill than climbing uphill. While reordering your life isn't always easy, the more authentic you become, the less dissatisfaction you will experience. Eventually, you'll wonder how you ever lived any other way.

"Creativity is connecting things. When you ask creative people how they did something, they feel a little guilty because they didn't really do it, they just saw something. It seemed obvious to them after a while. That's because they were able to connect experiences they've had and synthesize new things"

-Steve Jobs

As you explore and create,
it is important to reflect on
what you experience and learn.

Not everything you do will be
successful, satisfying and life affirming.

There will be paths which,
though they began with promise,
turn out to be dead ends.

Learning to more quickly recognize
your dissatisfaction with a given path
can save you from backtracking.

Reflection allows you to continually
monitor, measure and evaluate your happiness.

The act of reflecting,
of thinking about your experiences,
of weighing the various interpretations of those
experiences,
of revising your understanding of the world,
and integrating your insights,
allows you to sustain a happy life.

———————————

"The unexamined life is not worth living."

-Socrates

Reflect, Weigh, Evaluate, Integrate

As you explore, there will be days when you crest a ridge and find you can see both from whence you've come and where you're headed. Sit down, rest and enjoy the view. When you create, there will be times when you step back to view what you're fashioning. Don't get in a rush. Pause long enough to savor and marvel. These moments of reflection are crucial to sustaining a vibrant and satisfying life.

In the process of exploring and creating, you will encounter new ideas and insights. If you're wise, you'll take the time to reflect upon, weigh, evaluate and possibly integrate these ideas and insights into your understanding of the world. This is not a uniquely non-religious responsibility or activity. As a religious person – whether you sought them or not – you often encountered ideas or had insights that did not match your beliefs and assumptions. Though you may have been encouraged to ignore, discount or explain away these experiences, the fact you've read this far suggests you often took those ideas and insights seriously and spent time in reflection.

When it comes to reflection, the difference between the religious and non-religious approach to new ideas and insights is subtle, but significant. Though both religious and non-religious people are often reflective, there are differences in the motivation and process.

- The religious approach to reflection often seeks to maintain some equilibrium or defend the status quo while the non-religious approach may intentionally disturb it.
- Religious reflection relies on a single or primary source of authority while the non-religious method considers a multitude of possible authorities.
- The religious person is often taught to distrust personal intuition while the non-religious person tends to value or even rely on it.
- Though both styles make judgments, the religious approach often claims universal application while the non-religious is more focused on personal adjustments.

This table outlines these important distinctions.

Religious	Non-Religious
Reflect: Identify and define the new idea or insight.	
Weigh: Determine the religious opinion concerning the idea or insight. Distrust personal intuition.	**Weigh:** Explore the various opinions concerning the idea or insight. Value personal intuition.
Evaluate: Judge the idea or insight as universally right or wrong, good or evil.	**Evaluate:** Decide whether the idea or insight is personally helpful or satisfying
Integrate: Adopt ideas and insights with a positive evaluation	

If you've always used a non-religious reflection process, you may find none of this revolutionary and may want to skip the rest of this section. However, if the non-religious approach to reflection is alien to you, understanding and learning this process can be a significant and challenging shift. It takes time to develop and trust other sources of authority. Initially, you may feel uneasy or guilty for valuing your own intuition.

It can also be difficult to abandon the need for some absolute and universal determination of right or wrong or to stop applying your opinion to others. Give yourself time and practice as you learn to reflect differently about your life. Use the following exercise to help you reflect upon new ideas and insights.

A Reflection Exercise

As a post-religious person, you are encountering ideas you may not have previously considered. You are also having new insights about yourself and the world. Here are some ideas and insights of non-religious and post-religious people.

- My life belongs to me
- Many religious prohibitions should be ignored
- Scientific inquiry offers the best theories for most questions
- I am ultimately responsible for meeting my needs.
- There is no pre-determined plan for my life or design for the world
- Bad things happen randomly
- God does not exist
- When the evidence is inconclusive, my opinion is as valid as the opinion of anyone else
- There can be a multitude of right answers
- Forgiveness is an option rather than an obligation
- I cease to exist after I die
- Morality is a human construct
- I don't need anyone else to validate my existence
- I was born with incredible potential and possibility
- Mistakes are opportunities to mature
- I define the meaning for my life
- Caring for myself is not selfish

Take a moment and consider one of these ideas or insights. Choose one that has been recent and startling. If none of these are interesting, think about a recent idea you've encountered or a personal insight you've had. Write the idea or insight you've chosen in the space below:

Now ask yourself these questions.

1. What does your head or heart tell you about this idea or insight?

2. What sources of authority do you respect and trust in weighing it?

3. In what ways would adopting this idea or insight be helpful and satisfying?

4. In what ways would adopting this idea or insight be problematic?

5. How would you alter your life to integrate this idea or insight?

This exercise offers a model for reflecting on the new ideas and insights you encounter in life. As you develop confidence in determining what is personally compelling and helpful, you will find this process and its questions second nature. Eventually, you will develop a rhythm of exploration and creation followed by reflection and integration. In so doing, your life will become a well examined one – thoughtful, intentional and positive.

"By three methods we may learn wisdom;
first, by reflection, which is noblest;
second, by imitation, which is easiest;
and third, by experience, which is the bitterest."

-Confucius

Exploration, creation and reflection
need not be solitary endeavors.

Though the post-religious life
frees you to choose your own path,
it does not require you
to travel alone.

Indeed, you can travel with
or befriend whomever you choose.

No longer must you keep company with those
who look, act and think as you do.

You are free
to choose traveling companions
who've traveled where you've never been,
who've seen what you haven't seen,
and who've found happiness and satisfaction
in ways you never would have considered.

If you choose,
you can talk and listen to anyone.

Engage with those you find interesting.

Connect to those you find most helpful.

Befriend those who make you think and laugh.

Engage, Listen, Connect

Your contentment in life is often less about what you do and more about those with whom you do it. You can diminish the quality of your life if you only surround yourself with people who look, think and act exactly like you. While religions sometimes encourage or even command such conformity, you are now free to associate with anyone. There are no sinners or saints. Most people are living life as authentically as they are able. Once you understand this, nearly everyone you meet has something to offer and teach.

Often, those who differ from you the most can teach you the most. They guide you down paths you wouldn't have discovered on your own. They create what you wouldn't have thought of creating. Though you will certainly need people in your life who share your perspective, approach and values, remember the most successful explorers travel to foreign lands and meet exotic people.

Befriending people different than you – though important - is not the only consideration in choosing traveling companions. While they don't need to share your every opinion, they should respect your autonomy, value your perspective and share your wanderlust. Good traveling companions enjoy travel, whether it be of mind or body. Surrounding yourself with people who disdain exploration and creativity is a recipe for unhappiness.

In becoming a post-religious person, you are at one of those pivotal moments in life where the company you keep may change. Hopefully, you can see choosing new companions as an opportunity rather than a chore. The following suggestions may help you broaden your circle of acquaintances and friends. As always, try what seems interesting or helpful. Ignore what isn't authentic. Create what isn't offered.

- Sit down with your religious friends and explain your reasons for leaving your religious community. Try not to be self-righteous, judgmental, or evangelical. Ask them why their beliefs are still compelling. Celebrate their happiness as much as your own.

- Identify one of your deepest passions and interests. Research what groups and organizations share this passion and interest. Visit one of their meetings. Introduce yourself to one or two people and engage in conversation. See if they could provide community or companionship.

- Gather a small group of people with diverse experiences and backgrounds to discuss some existential question, social issue or psychological challenge. Make it a dinner party. Collect a different set of people and discuss something provocative.

- Join or create a book club with the focus on books that provoke thought and challenge assumptions.

- Find a provocative blog or social network. Participate in dialogue and discussion. The internet has made it possible to connect with people across diverse religions, cultures and viewpoints.

- Go on a personal retreat. Find some place where you can be alone. Take good books and music. Journal. Take a long walk or a long bath. Spend some quality time with yourself.

- Keep your head up during public prayer and make eye contact with others who aren't bowing their heads. If you know them, seek them out and ask them about their motivation.

- Identify an important cause and advance it. Research what is being done and who is doing significant work. Give your time as well as your money. Connect with other people who care about the cause as deeply as you do. Ask them why and listen to them.

- Find a writer or thinker who views the world as you do. Read everything they've written in chronological order. Notice how their thoughts and opinions evolve. Go hear them speak if possible.

- Find a writer or thinker who views the world very differently than you. Read something they've written rather than what has been written about them. Try to understand why they understand the world the way they do.

The post-religious life need not be a solitary one. Though there will be moments when you travel or camp alone, far more often you will find yourself sharing your journey with others. Be curious about where they've been and what they've seen. Consider their unique perspective on the world. Be open to all they have to teach you.

"At bottom every man knows well enough that he is a unique being, only once on this earth; and by no extraordinary chance will such a marvelously picturesque piece of diversity in unity as he is, ever be put together a second time."

-Friedrich Nietzsche

From a non-religious point of view,
first and foremost,
you will always be a student.

From the day of your birth
until the day you die,
you will collect information,
experiment and learn
about the world.

You will explore, create, reflect and engage
in order to better understand yourself.

Though you need never quit being a student,
at some point in the journey
you will also become a teacher.

Those coming behind you,
traveling paths you once walked
and exploring places you've been,
will ask for your story.

You will have opportunities
to share your experiences and opinions
about life, meaning and purpose
with many,
especially your own children.

Share, Explain, Teach

Sharing and explaining your opinions about yourself and the world can be challenging as a post-religious person. You can leave your religious tradition, abandon most of its beliefs and still largely retain a religious approach to interpersonal interaction and parenting. You may have to break some bad habits.

As a religious person, you were probably taught to understand truth as something you possessed. Your shared this truth – asked or unasked – with as many people as possible, hoping to convince and recruit them. When possible, you may have felt perfectly comfortable imposing your opinions on others. Those who ignored or rejected your appeals and opinions were pitied at best and condemned at worst.

When it came to your children, as a religious person, you had the responsibility of raising them in the faith. You indoctrinated them when they were most malleable, assuring their adherence to your religion's beliefs and practices. This indoctrination, though inappropriate from a non-religious perspective, was the religious equivalent of a vaccination. You were protecting your children from ideas and experiences that might destroy them. To do otherwise was irresponsible.

If you were once religious, though you may no longer think you possess the truth or you must guard your children from worldly perspectives, you may find yourself approaching your interactions with a religious bent. It can be helpful as you relate to others – especially to those over whom you have power - to remember these non-religious, interpersonal values.

1. No single person possesses all the answers. Indeed, truth is illusive and forever evolving. What is thought true today, may not prove true tomorrow.

2. Truth is a puzzle. While humanity has some of the pieces, many are still missing. Claiming to see the whole picture is

arrogant and self-limiting. If you know it all, there is no further need to explore or create.

3. Everyone has an opinion. When given unasked, it is rude and disrespectful. It is also seldom embraced. When asked for and humbly shared, it has value. It is usually seriously considered.

4. Imposing your opinion on others violates their autonomy. The need for coercion often demonstrates the inadequacy of an idea.

5. If your opinion has merit, others will be attracted to it. Your sole responsibility is sharing and explaining your opinion as clearly as possible.

6. Allowing others the freedom, time and space to come to their own conclusions and opinions is a sign of respect.

When you remember these values in your interactions with others you invite them to journey with you. You offer openness, curiosity and adventure rather than the religious certainties of the past. You demonstrate your confidence in their ability to handle ambiguity, explore and create. There is no need to recruit or indoctrinate.

This can be freeing for a parent. You don't have to have all the answers. You don't have to protect your children from alternate ideas. Allowing them to explore, create, reflect, make mistakes and ultimately determine their own path isn't irresponsible. It is an act of love and respect. When they ask tough questions, telling them you don't know and asking their opinion allows them to embrace a world where certainty is no longer the highest value. It also creates space for them to form their own opinion.

As in previous sections, the following suggestions are offered as starting points for sharing your journey, experiences and opinions with those around you. As with every previous list, try what sounds interesting and ignore the rest.

- Curb your enthusiasm about the non-religious life. Try not to insert your opinions into conversations. Resist the need to correct the opinions of others. However, when asked, offer your opinion unapologetically.

- Consider joining an organization like the American Humanist Association, the Center For Inquiry or the Council for Secular Humanism. These organizations offer many opportunities to learn and teach. Many people asking for information about a non-religious life begin their inquiry with such groups.

- Start a blog. Write about your journey, experiences and opinions. Invite others to subscribe.

- Sit down with friends and family who are struggling with their religious affiliation. Ask open ended questions about their struggle. Only offer your opinion and story when asked.

- When asked your religious affiliation, identify as non-religious. When people seem genuinely interested, explain your decision to become non-religious. Ask them how they identify themselves and if they're happy.

- If you are a parent, read *Raising Free Thinkers: A Practical Guide for Parenting Beyond Belief.* This book offers practical advice and activities for raising open minded children. As a religious parent, you may have relied on the tradition to train your children. This is now wholly your responsibility.

- Expose your children to a rich diversity of opinion and thought. Teach them how to reflect after mind expanding experiences.

- Make certain your children are familiar with the great world religions and their beliefs and practices. Visit religious settings and services. Allow them to develop their own conclusions about the value and inadequacies of religion.

- Connect your children with other children from post or non-religious households. Make certain they have friends and acquaintances who are creating lives outside a religious context.

The goal of the post-religious life is not to convince others to become post or non- religious. Your greatest challenge will always be living your life as authentically as you can. If you continually and visibly strive for authenticity, this is also your greatest gift to your children. In watching you, they will learn to construct and modify a happy and satisfying life. They will never need to read this book. Your example will be enough.

"As a parent, it's my responsibility to equip my child to do this - to grieve when grief is necessary and to realize that life is still profoundly beautiful and worth living despite the fact that we inevitably lose one another and that life ends, and we don't know what happens after death."

-Sam Harris

When you were religious,
time was set aside for
rest, inspiration and celebration.

You were encouraged
to pause, relax, rest and reflect.

There were events that inspired and delighted,
moving you emotionally and lifting your spirits.

There was pomp and circumstance,
pageantry and poetry,
song and dance.

When you became post-religious,
you lost the carefully orchestrated experiences
provided by religion.

You did not lose your need or ability
to relax, delight or celebrate.

As you explore and create,
rest and relax,
delight in the wonderful,
be inspired by the transcendent,
celebrate this adventure
called life.

Relax, Delight, Celebrate

Religions create space for rest and relaxation. Prayer, worship and other religious activities provide an escape from the daily grind of life. The setting aside of time for rest, personal reflection, communal gathering and family interaction is universally beneficial. When religion is at its best, it protects you from filling every hour with business and distraction. At its worst, it can become drudgery.

As a post-religious person, rest and relaxation remain healthy practices. You may want to purposely keep the times you once spent in religious services, practices or events as time to rest, relax, reflect and celebrate. If you were a faithful religious adherent, you easily spent ten to fifteen hours a week in religious activities. If you were involved in religious leadership, you may have spent even more time

When these activities brought you happiness, they were time well spent. Unfortunately, if you continued those activities after they became meaningless, you were wasting time. Being post-religious frees up many hours previously spent on religion.

Though leaving can initially create a void, it can also feel like a vacation. Every day has an additional hour or two. Some evenings may be available for new activity or relaxation. No longer do you arrange your life around a religious calendar. Weekends are freed for family, travel or rest. The often hectic routine of preparing for and attending religious services is replaced with whatever brings you peace – sleeping, reading, exercising, playing or love making. If the religious knew what the non-religious were doing while they were in worship, churches, temples and mosques might empty.

Though the post-religious can certainly fill up their lives with obligations or distractions as easily as the religious, when you first leave a religious community there is a wonderful opportunity for reordering your time in ways that bring you more happiness and satisfaction. Resist filling the void too quickly. Think carefully about how to use this time

When you were religious, you were asked to be a good steward of your time, to use it effectively to advance a religious cause. As a steward, the implication was that your time belonged to God and you were accountable for each and every minute. As a post-religious person, your time belongs to you. When you use it for yourself, it is self-care and not selfishness. When you give it to others, it is a gift and not a requirement.

How you define a good use of your time is completely up to you. Don't let others determine how you use or value this limited resource. If the afterlife is uncertain, every day should be treasured. Generally, if what you are doing is improving the quality of your life or making the world a better place, it is never a waste of time. If what you're doing leaves you exhausted or unhappy, something is deeply wrong.

Inspire and Delight

Religions are skilled at creating experiences that inspire and delight. They use architecture, pageantry, language, music, poetry and story to create moments when people feel especially connected to each other, the world and their inner self. You may have fond memories of moments in your religious life when you were emotionally moved, intellectually inspired and overwhelmed with gratitude.

When you were religious, you depended upon your religious community orchestrating emotionally powerful moments. Indeed, your satisfaction with your religious experience was probably closely correlated with its creation of such moments. If the religious events you attended became dry and lifeless, you probably looked elsewhere for inspiration.

As a post-religious person, you still seek inspiration and delight. You simply seek it in many places, experiences and moments. The following list offers some suggestions for creating and inviting moments of transcendence.

- Find buildings or places where you are awed or moved by their grandeur or ambiance. A museum, a library, a garden, a park. Visit this spot when you need inspiration.

- Designate certain days or moments for pomp and circumstance. Dress up. Wear a hat. Make what you're doing into a special event.

- Find music that moves you deeply. Create a soundtrack for special events or occasions. Attend concerts.

- Attend live theatre. Choose plays or musicals that explore the human condition, that inspire you to live more fully. There is power is sharing such moments with hundreds of other people.

- Read poetry aloud and with others. It can be non-religious liturgy. Memorize poems that inspire and delight.

- Explore nature. Nothing connects you to yourself better than exploring your connection with the universe.

- Spend time with young children. They are pre-religious and see the world in ways you've forgotten. They delight in things you take for granted. See the world through their eyes.

In whatever you do, be observant, looking for the unusual and extraordinary. There will be times when you are once again overwhelmed by the wonder of it all. You will connect to the universe in ways you can't describe, be inspired to live your life more fully. What you are experiencing is what humans have always experienced, even before religions gave it a name and source. You are experiencing the transcendent.

Celebrate

Religions do a good job of creating celebratory moments. As a post-religious person, replacing such occasions can be daunting. You may be drawn back to religion during religious holidays or celebrations. You may miss the pageantry, music or liturgy. When you grow nostalgic, it's helpful to remember you've not lost the ability to celebrate. You've simply lost your most recent excuse.

Celebration predates religion. Whenever life has been especially good, or there has been a significant shift in daily rhythm, or people wanted to remember and honor some past person or event, there has been celebration. Religious celebrations often piggybacked on ancient festivals, offering adherents a substitute for the non-religious celebrations they previously valued and enjoyed.

For example, Christmas was clearly an attempt by the early Church to offer a substitute for the traditional Winter solstice festivals in many cultures. Christmas trees, yule logs, ham dinners and gift giving all have their roots in these ancient celebrations. Easter coincidently falls during the ancient spring fertility celebrations. The Jewish holiday Purim – with children dressing up as ancient Jewish heroes and asking for candy door to door - looks like Halloween. Halloween or All Hallows Eve falls on the night of an ancient Celtic celebration. Ramadan is pre-dated by an ancient Arabic festival that involved fasting followed by feasting. The list goes on and on.

As a post-religious person, celebration can continue to be an important and exciting part of your life. Births, coming of age, marriages and death all need to be celebrated or honored. People have been doing this for thousands of years, long before your religion or any other religion existed. The following list offers suggestions on sustaining or even enhancing the celebratory moments of life.

- Think about the religious holidays you once celebrated. If some of these holidays were especially enjoyable or meaningful, identify the elements you most enjoyed. Were they inherently religious? If not, continue enjoying those elements. If some of these practices now feel inauthentic, create your own variations. Sing different songs. Read different poetry. Tell different stories.

- Think about the secular holidays you presently celebrate. If some of these holidays are especially enjoyable or meaningful, focus your energy, planning and money on celebrating them.

- Create celebrations around important events, issues and people in your life. Do something special on these days with others who share these values.

- Explore the many events, moments and reasons different cultures celebrate. If you know your ancestry, research what your ancestors would have celebrated. Look for celebrations that resonate with your values and passions.

- Celebrate global holidays like Earth Day and Human Rights Day. Create your own ritual or celebration as a family or individual.

- Babies can still be treasured. Marriage can still be celebrated. The dead can still be honored. None of these moments require a religious framework. Be creative.

- Think about how you wish to be remembered when you die. Write down your wishes. Make certain your non-religious status is respected when you die. Record a personal message you'd like played at your memorial service.

If you live your life well, there will be much to celebrate. If you treat life as an adventure, there will be much that inspires and delights. If you live fully, you will need to take time to relax and marvel at your wonderful life. It is most wonderful when you discover the potential of each moment to take your breath away.

"You only live once, but if you do it right, once is enough."

-Mae West

The end of this book is merely a beginning.

As a non-religious person,
there is no destination,
no ending point,
and no finish line.

There is simply another path to take,
another place to visit, another experience to savor.

Exploration and creation,
reflection and integration,
engagement and connection,
inspiration and celebration,
are the steps of the journey.

You are not who you were.

You have become who you want to be,
at this time and in this place.

When it is necessary, you will change again.
Until then, have fun.

"Here is a test to find out whether your mission in life is complete.
If you're alive, it isn't."

-Richard Bach

About the Author

James Mulholland was raised in the conservative Christian evangelical tradition. He pastored Methodist and Quaker congregations for over twenty-five years. He wrote three best-selling books on practical theology and was a popular public speaker. In 2008, Jim resigned his pastorate and began walking away from religion.

For more information about Jim, his personal story and his continued journey, please visit LeavingYourReligion.com.

CPSIA information can be obtained at www.ICGtesting.com
Printed in the USA
LVOW11s0236141213

365264LV00018B/977/P